THE POWER TO STOP

Stopping as a Path to Self-love,
Personal Power and Enlightenment

Extraordinary Praise For
THE POWER TO STOP

Karen Bentley's inspiring book, *The Power to Stop*, is just that: **inspiring**. What does the word inspiring mean? It implies that this is a book that shows a path to connection with Spirit. It is a book that tells me that without connecting to Spirit, without welcoming the Love within, there is no way to be free from limiting beliefs and self-sabotaging behavior.

Karen Bentley's life story is a demonstration of the fact that spirit heals. Ms. Bentley's book gives the reader not only the blueprint for the journey to joy, it lays out the blueprint with infectious passion. If there be a healing message, what heals more than anything else is the sheet conviction of the one who delivers the message. It is **conviction** that jumps off every page of *The Power to Stop*. It is conviction which infuses every line with certainty. This conviction is the result of Knowing. Knowing is the result of deep introspection and the removal of barriers to Love. The only way to heal is to remove the barriers I have erected against Love.

In *The Power to Stop*, Karen Bentley brilliantly lays out a joyful and inspiring "how to." Has she herself removed all barriers? No. She does not claim to be enlightened. She makes no claim of Guru status. She very lovingly suggests that she is on the path with you and that she Knows this path is transforming her life as it will yours. She has no doubt. And knowing this work and knowing the passion Karen brings to this work I, too, have no doubt.

Anyone who struggles with substance issues, anyone who uses food to punish himself, anyone whose self-sabotage prevents the experience of true joy, peace and love, will find that *The Power to Stop* is truly a gem. You have this little book in your hands now…make the decision. You can do it and, more importantly, you are worth it!

Diederik Wolsak
RPC, MPCP, Program Director
Choose Again Attitudinal Healing Centers
Costa Rica and Vancouver, BC
www.choose-again.com

Following any spiritual path or healing path needs one important component, the willingness to practice it. Talking about making changes in your life and actually making those changes are two different ideas. Here in this book Karen Bentley gives you easy, concrete steps to make the changes that become a testament to loving yourself whole-HEARTedly. Karen walks with you as one who has been there in the seemingly unstoppable behavior, an honest equal, who is now a loving guide who encourages you to be your authentic self as you release the chains that bind. *The Power to Stop* is within you. Embrace it, and it will embrace you.

Revs. Deborah and Paul Phelps
Founders, Miracles One Foundation Church
www.miraclesone.org

Stop. Read this book, *The Power to Stop*. Dedicate yourself to a love-based 30-day program. What behaviors in your life do you need to stop? Drinking alcohol? Binge eating? Promiscuity and risky sex? You **can** stop and Karen Bentley will help you. Or should I say "Cairn" Bentley like those Scottish piles of rocks that tell you which way to go. Feeling guilty about your addictive past and wasted life opportunities? Stop. You don't think you have "the power to stop." Stop that thinking. You do have the power, and now you have the tools. You also have an experienced coach, Karen Bentley.

Rev. Tony Ponticello
Author, *After Enlightenment*
Co-founder, Community Miracles Center
www.miracles-course.org

The Power to Stop is truly a treasure that will change your life. In this book Karen Bentley teaches ways to practice transcending the ego's impulse to self-destruct. She shows you how to use your innate God-given power in the present moment to choose the Voice for God. We highly recommend this book!

Robert and Mary Stoelting
Co-founders of Pathways of Light
www.pathwaysoflight.org

Developing a spiritual practice that can consistently restore us to the Truth is perhaps THE most important thing we can do in our lives. So many people are content with knowing wonderful spiritual sayings and truths. The problem is, understanding and believing the truth doesn't really take us very far. Learning to integrate, choose and embody the Truth that we are in each moment is where the rubber meets the road, and that has nothing to do with belief.

The Power to Stop is designed to transform your spiritual understandings into a living reality. It's well written, funny, engaging, effective and practical. If you're truly ready to take the next step in living what you know to be True in your heart, now is the time to pick up this wonderful book and follow its instruction. If you do, I know your life will never be the same.

David Paul Doyle
Author, *5 Steps to Hearing God's Voice*
Co-founder, The Voice for Love
www.thevoiceforlove.com

I love Karen Bentley. She glows. I am personally inspired by her beautiful example in helping people to access their power to stop any addictive behavior. This book is a miracle. Karen is upbeat, and this book is written in a fun way that really encouraged me to stick with the 30-day program. This book is a guide that can help anyone stop any out-of-control behavior, with some very simple practical tools to clear out the clutter in your head, in your life (and probably your fridge and cupboards, too.) This is a beautiful book that can change your life.

Lisa Natoli
Author, *Gorgeous for God*
www.gorgeousforgod.com

Sign me up! I had the chance to read your work today and am motivated to begin a practice of refraining and not doing. I am a disciplined doer and love the idea of becoming a disciplined undoer. Your approach toward healing and addiction is organically solid, but I believe *The Power to Stop* holds a greater gift for living each day, the power of awareness and conscious choice. It reads like a recipe to end denial, the enemy of lovers of Truth.

I especially like that Spirit is an integral part of your solution. The references to Castaneda and ACIM evidence a thoughtfulness that will take your readers far beyond thirty days, (dare I say it?) into eternal mindscapes. The program promises a compelling mix of mysticism, shamanism, practicality, metaphysics, Love, big-hearted zeal and chicken soup: gifts and lessons for the soul that truly desires freedom.

If anyone can make "stop" appealing, it's you dear Karen, master of abstinence and lover of the fullness of the unfettered life. I am determined to go stop now. I mean to stop going now...

MaryBeth Scalice, MA, EdD
Author, *The Love of Your Life: The Jesse and Lily Intimacies Volume 1*
www.marybethscalice.com

Finally, a book that offers a quick and effective way to stop those destructive behavior patterns we all struggle with. I know. Other books have made this claim, but *The Power to Stop* really delivers! Imagine being able to master that lifelong behavior in only 30 days! The instructions to accomplish this marvelous feat are simple yet powerful, combining basic psychology with profound spiritual wisdom.

This is the book you have always hoped to find, and you will want to buy several copies to share with friends and family. I'm making my list of lucky recipients right now.

Rev. Myron Jones
Author, *Healing Family Relationships* and *Hey, Holy Spirit, It's Me Again*
Pathways of Light Minister
www.forgivenessthewayhome.org

Anyone who wants renewed hope and specific, how-to guidance on changing a habit will benefit from this book. *The Power to Stop* is affirming and uplifting...like a visit with a dear friend.

Author, *Create A Life that Tickles Your Soul* and *Recharge In Minutes*
Motivational Speaker, Writer, Coach
www.zoglio.com

A truly creative, one-of-a-kind application of the principles of *A Course In Miracles*. This very specific 30-dayprogram defies all our expectations for how to gain control of addictive behaviors. Karen affirms our power, tells us to use it, not to manifest our dreams but to *stop*. She extols self-love and refuses to motivate with guilt, yet guides us to say no to even culturally approved self-indulgence. She praises the innate spirit within us, yet has us express that spirit by refusing our ego in ways we've been told simply can't be done. People often ask me how to deal with their addictions in a way that reflects *A Course In Miracles*. Aside from pointing them to certain sections, I haven't had much to say. Now I can point to this book.

Robert Perry
Founder, Circle of Atonement
www.circleofa.org

Simply put, "the ego is not the Self." Thinking that something which is not of God can have power over us, leads us down an unpleasant path of despair. Karen Bentley's new book, *The Power to Stop* is a potent tool in helping us to bring an end to insane ego thinking, choose once again and follow God's plan for salvation.

Jon Mundy, PhD
Author, *Living A Course In Miracles*
Publisher, *Miracles Magazine*
www.miraclesmagazine.org

In *The Power to Stop* we are gently reminded of the Light of Christ within each of us. Karen Bentley walks with us on our loving kindness quest to our spiritual destination and we become witnesses to her conversations with the Voice of the Holy Spirit, and feel the guidance of her mighty companions, our brothers Carlos Castaneda and Jesus.

In reading Karen's words I am reminded of one of my favorite passages in *A Course In Miracles:* "Those who are certain of the outcome can afford to wait, and wait without anxiety. Patience is natural to the teacher of God. All he sees is certain outcome, at a time perhaps unknown to him as yet, but not in doubt."

So no matter how many 30-day journeys we may take… as we allow Karen to take us on this journey remember to be patient, gentle and…trust! Know the outcome is certain and will lead us to our Christ-self.

Sharon Sherrard
Co-founder, A Center For Inner Peace
www.acenterforinnerpeace.org

Much applause for Karen Bentley's *The Power to Stop*. Having been a long-time advocate of the application of spiritual discipline as taught in *A Course In Miracles, The Power to Stop* offers anyone an introduction into the powerful life-changing benefits when the choice is made to change perception.

I was very honestly impressed with your work. The world needs more like you. Bravo Karen!

Joe Wolfe
Author, *The End of Reincarnation with the Five Signs* and *Letter to a Prisoner*
Founder of Spirit Light Outreach Speaker
www.spiritlightoutreach.org

Karen Bentley is one of my author clients with a big heart and a powerful, inspiring message. She brings much-needed hope to anyone who thinks they can't end a behavior which has become a bad habit or destructive addiction.

Steve Harrison
RADIO-TV INTERVIEW REPORT, the magazine producers read to find guests
www.rtir.com

ACIM is a gift for all mankind, a gift that can be applied to all the challenges of life. *The Course* can be summarized as a three-step forgiveness process where one faces the wrong-minded situation, recalls our perfection as the Perfect Child of God that we are; and then turns the situation over to the Holy Spirit with no strings attached.

Karen Bentley has given us a wonderful book to help us stop out-of-control behavior based on this forgiveness process and has done so in easy-to-follow plain language.

Bob LeRoy
President, Open Doors Classroom for the Universal Course
www.opendoorsclassroom.com

THE POWER TO STOP

any OUT-OF-CONTROL
BEHAVIOR IN 30 DAYS

Stopping as a Path to Self-love,
Personal Power and Enlightenment

KAREN BENTLEY

NEW YORK

THE POWER TO STOP
any OUT-OF-CONTROL BEHAVIOR IN 30 DAYS

Stopping as a Path to Self-love, Personal Power and Enlightenment

by KAREN BENTLEY

ISBN: 978-1-61448-190-4
Library of Congress Control Number: 2011945521

Published by:
Morgan James Publishing
The Entrepreneurial Publisher
5 Penn Plaza, 23rd Floor
New York City, New York 10001
(212) 655-5470 Office
(516) 908-4496 Fax
www.MorganJamesPublishing.com

www.powertostop.com
www.stopoutofcontroleating.com
www.stoppingnation.com

Cover Design by:
Rachel Lopez
www.r2cdesign.com

Interior Design by:
Bonnie Bushman
bbushman@bresnan.net

In an effort to support local communities, raise awareness and funds, Morgan James Publishing donates a percentage of all book sales for the life of each book to Habitat for Humanity Peninsula and Greater Williamsburg.
Get involved today, visit
www.MorganJamesBuilds.com.

People hardly ever realize that we can cut anything from our lives, any time, just like that. He snapped his fingers.

Do you think that one can stop smoking or drinking that easily? I asked.

Sure! he said with great conviction. *Smoking and drinking are nothing. Nothing at all if we want to drop them.*

…He said there was only one thing which was indispensible for anything we did. He called it "the spirit."

One can't do without the spirit, he said. *And you don't have it. Worry about that…*

Carlos Castaneda
JOURNEY TO IXTLAN

TABLE OF CONTENTS

Recognize that what has no effects does not exist.

A COURSE IN MIRACLES

WEEK FOUR

WEEK FIVE

PREFACE

Quotes and meditations

The Power to Stop is deeply inspired by *A Course In Miracles*, also known by the acronym ACIM, which was first published in the 1970's and by a series of books written by Carlos Castaneda from 1968 to 1998. Both of these works offer a complete system of thinking that leads to the undoing of the ego and harmlessness to self and others. Quotes and meditation phrases from ACIM are used in each of the 30-day lessons, and ideas from both Castaneda and ACIM have been adapted and used throughout *The Power to Stop*. There is no need to read either of these works or to even be familiar with them. Introductory information about *A Course In Miracles* is provided in Day 29, and a brief overview of Castaneda and his work is provided in Day 30.

References to Christ

The word *Christ* is used in a non-denominational, non-religious way to describe the wholly loving, sacred consciousness that dwells within us all and connects us to God and to each other. If preferred, you are welcome to substitute other words for this consciousness such as Spirit, Source, Light, God, Goddess, Creator, Holy Spirit or whatever term is familiar and more comfortable to you. *The Power to Stop* is not connected to any religion or group. It's completely independent and teaches reliance on wisdom from within.

How to read this book

After reading the introductory material, please read the rest of the book one day at a time for 30 consecutive days. If you feel the need to stay with a particular lesson for a longer period of time, do so. Only take one lesson per day.

The Power to Stop is not a medical program

The Power to Stop is not a medical program, and no medical advice is given or intended. Extreme withdrawal situations which may be life-threatening are beyond the scope of *The Power to Stop* and are not addressed. Note that *The Power to Stop* involves daily physical activity. Anyone with a pre-existing health condition, physical limitations, or physical concerns of any kind should check with their physician before beginning the program. *The Power to Stop* does not replace or override the advice of your physician.

LOVE LETTER TO READERS

Dear Reader,

Just when you think you've read every book and heard every conceivable sound byte about out-of-control behaviors, addictions and compulsions, out comes a message and a simple daily process so exhilarating it takes your breath away. You've been seeking a new solution, and this is it. There are no coincidences.

The Power to Stop is organized and presented in a way that releases you from fears about your out-of-control behavior or your inability to stop yourself. The total absence of fear-based ideas will present a radically different message for most people. We live in a fear-based world where fear is erroneously perceived as correct, useful and godly. Since I do not extend any ideas that engender fear, it's not reasonable to expect the same old message about stopping that you've heard a thousand times before.

The process of learning how to stop yourself is also the deeply calming practice of learning how to love yourself. This uncompromising love-based solution makes *The Power to Stop* a miracle in action. Miracles are possible because the Holy Spirit is present whenever love is extended and received, especially love of self. You are worthy of a healing miracle. You are worthy of self-love and the love of others. You are worthy of goodness. You are worthy of having the life and bodily experience that you envision for yourself.

The Power to Stop is the uplifting message that I personally most wanted to hear, but could not find anywhere else except inside myself. It's with great joy and humble service to the world that I share this song in my heart that *must* be sung.

Love is the only thing that really matters,

Karen Bentley

HELP YOURSELF

No one can do your push-ups for you

The strength to do comes from your undivided decision.
A COURSE IN MIRACLES

G*o get help*. It's a familiar mantra, isn't it? Don't get me wrong, I'm not suggesting that getting help is bad or inappropriate because it's not. Individuals and groups that help others play a useful and important role. Countless people have been helped by 12-step programs, rehab facilities, psychotherapists, psychologists, clinicians, and coaches and counselors of every kind. Lives have been saved and personal direction has been changed. I make no judgment, whatsoever, about providing or using any of these helping services. After all, I am providing one.

Helpers are blessed with the power to inspire. They provide living examples. They focus intense knowledge and attention on a problem. They provide fellowship and joining in common purpose. They can be a source of joy, but aren't always. This is a monumental boost, and I aspire to provide this kind of jump-start to you. Yet in the midst of all this well-intended help, it's possible to forget your active role in the stopping process. Your decision to stop and to heal lays the foundation for any form of help you receive.

The all-consuming focus our society places on *getting help* distracts you from realizing that you have the power to stop on your own, and it makes doing-it-yourself seem unlikely. But it's not. Not at all. Keep in mind, no one gives you inner

2

peace. No one gives you personal power. No one connects you to your Christ-self. And no one stops for you, either. Stopping is entirely up to you.

Here's another thought. What if you wait and wait and wait and wait for help, but no one comes to save you? The Navy SEALs might be busy with other things. Your spouse or significant other might be too sick of your nonsense to care. Your parents might be dead or out of resources. Your children are more concerned with their own lives than fixing yours. Your counselor might be well intended but useless. You might not have a convenient group or a group with a happy message. Maybe all you have to rely on is yourself and the Christ that dwells within. Is this *really* such a terrible, frightening thing?

Relatives, friends, groups and service providers may care deeply for you, and they may have really good, relevant information to share. But they don't know more about you than you. And they can't make a stopping decision for you. Not now, not ever. That's your job. When you rely on others for basic decision-making, you create even more neediness and dependency, and this is one of the problems you're trying to solve. Giving your power away also leads to the misperception that you *must* get help rather than the idea that you're using it as an *optional* tool. It's a subtle but important and empowering distinction.

If you want the advice or service of an expert, get it. If you prefer social connections and support groups, get that too. If it makes it easier for you to participate in a formal program or to have a coach, find one. Educate yourself. Gather opinions. Learn new skills. Give yourself whatever you think you need to achieve your own peak performance. Go back as many times as necessary for information or assistance, but always remember one thing. It's your decision at work, and that decision is an act of power.

The biggest favor I have to offer is to encourage you to recognize your own power and honor it.

THE REVOLUTIONARY DIFFERENCE

Transcend your ego

Errors are of the ego, and correction of errors
lies in the relinquishment of the ego.
A COURSE IN MIRACLES

Every unwanted, out-of-control behavior comes from the same ego-based impulse to self-destruct. *The Power to Stop* is radically and dramatically different from all other stopping programs because it recognizes this destructive impulse as the root cause of the problem and teaches how to *override* or *transcend* it.

Anything that weakens and destroys you is not your friend. Ego is not your friend, and it cannot be improved to morph into a friend. Yet, a strong and robust ego is universally cultivated and valued. The messages you hear in our world are ego messages. They revolve around the importance of ego and the things you can do to give it support and keep it propped up. This daily conditioning and messaging is relentless, trapping you in the belief that ego is important and essential for a happy, successful life.

The Power to Stop teaches how to break free of the ego trap. It presents you with another message and another support system, one that Wills you to live. This resource is your Christ-self, and it's the Source of all strength, all wisdom and right action. The Christ is always available to you. *The Power to Stop* teaches how to withdraw attention and energy from the ego and transfer it to the Christ-self.

The specific process of learning how to make this energy transfer is achieved by undoing an ordinary, unwanted behavior. The behavior becomes a practical grounding tool that provides much needed focus and inspiration. Even more, it accelerates spiritual growth and makes it more efficient. Formless goals of self-love, personal power and moments of enlightenment are otherwise too abstract and lacking in system or discipline for most people to achieve.

The Castaneda series that I told you about in the Preface is worth reading because it exposes the ego as a *foreign installation*. I really like this terminology because it puts you on alert that the ego is a predator, and it reminds you that God did not create you with an ego. We know for sure that ego does not come from God because ego is not eternal. It can be temporarily and permanently disengaged. When ego is disengaged, even if it's just for a moment, you are enlightened. The moment the ego is turned off, the Christ-self *must* come through. There's no way to stop it. That's why all that you need is a moment of enlightenment to stop yourself.

START THE COUNTDOWN

30 days to self-love, personal power and enlightenment

Increasing motivation for change in the learner is
all that a teacher need do to guarantee change.
A COURSE IN MIRACLES

Earlier this year my girlfriend Gina took her first Zumba class, and ever since then she's turned into a raving Zumba fan who can't resist telling and retelling me all about it every time we get together. For those of you who don't hang out in fitness clubs, Zumba is a kind of vigorous dance/exercise class with a sassy Latino flair. But why, you might rightly ask, are we talking about Zumba and what does it possibly have to do with stopping? Please indulge me for a minute, and you'll find out.

Being a sixty-something woman, Gina could easily play the age card and find an excuse to avoid a high energy program like Zumba. Instead of whining about how hard it is to keep up with the younger girls, Gina says she just makes the moves easier and keeps going. No one cares that she's the oldest person in the class. No one cares that she doesn't do all the steps perfectly. No one cares that her bootie doesn't shimmy and shake on command. Gina's participation is the only thing that counts. She enjoys participating, and she gets something from it.

Even though she claims to be the lowest and slowest performing student, Gina's participation makes it possible for her to extract the maximum benefit from her Zumba class. Like Gina, you have to participate to get the maximum benefit from

The Power to Stop. Participation is the big secret of your stopping success. This is the one rule you have to follow right from the start.

> You learn stopping by *practicing* stopping, not by reading about stopping.
>
> You restore excitement and passion to your life by *practicing* stopping, not by reading about stopping.
>
> You develop personal power and inner strength by *practicing* stopping, not by reading about stopping.

Get the idea? Nothing will happen without your active, fully engaged participation. Nothing. *Forget about sitting back and having a passive reading experience.* You have to feel the heat and the force of life in your veins, and the only way that happens is through the osmosis of participation. At the end of this chapter I'll be asking you to make a firm decision to fully participate in *The Power to Stop* program for the next 30 days. Don't make the decision yet. Pause a moment. Listen. Consider. Allow me the exquisite pleasure of seducing you with the prospect of your own self-love and your own personal power. Remember, 30 days is all you have to ask of yourself. It's all you have to do. In terms of your lifespan, it's the blink of an eye.

Containing the stopping experience to a 30-day period is a deliberate strategy to release fears and blockages around the stopping process. It's a subtle way of giving yourself full permission to play in the stopping space and to take big, bold, exuberant steps instead of tiny, hesitant ones. And it's smart, too, because when you directly experience stopping, you realize it's not the big bad deal you make it out to be in your head. Ditch all those grim-faced, emotionally-draining ideas you have about stopping yourself. This will <u>not</u> be your stopping experience. I promise.

Don't think beyond the 30-day period. Nothing good comes from brooding about the future and worrying about what you'll do after the program is over. Let the future take care of itself. Your job is to get excited about what you're doing now. Do you feel the spark of rejuvenation? Is there a hopeful thought in your mind? Hold that thought.

Here's what you get for your modest but consistent 30-day investment of effort in self.

♥ In just 30 days from today you'll break free of a habit that brings you down, makes you feel bad about yourself, and blocks your happiness. Your happiness is the most important thing in the world and cannot be sacrificed for any reason.

♥ In just 30 days from today you'll directly experience yourself as a loving, powerful being by communing with your Christ-self and mining power from your Christ-self. The power is already there, but you have to bring it to the forefront of your life and use it.

♥ In just 30 days from today you'll restore your purpose and passion for being alive. Your life is precious and you are here on planet Earth for a reason. What is it? How can you begin to more fully express your purpose every single day instead of stifling your own creative desire?

♥ In just 30 days from today, you'll experience inner peace and calmness without the food, substance, or behavior you now think you need so badly. Peace, which is *not doing*, is one of the skills to be learned and is an important part in your healing.

♥ In just 30 days from today you'll look better because you're taking better care of yourself. Improved appearance is the natural and ordinary by-product of self-love. Children who are taken care of are loved. Houses that are taken care of are loved. You will take care of yourself as a tangible demonstration of your love for self.

♥ In just 30 days from today you'll realize that non-romantic love is the answer to every problem in the world, including this one. You will be the love you seek. You will treat yourself with love, and you will extend your love to others. This love has nothing to do with many social practices that pass for love. Rather, it is the love that is your Truth, and you *do* want it.

Okay, so here's the deal with stopping. Any unwanted habit can be stopped: out-of-control eating, binge drinking, smoking, drugging, mindless sexing, excessive shopping – you name it, and it can be stopped. No exceptions! You probably think your particular stopping problem is worse than someone else's, harder to stop than someone else's, or just plain more troublesome than someone else's, but it isn't. Every stopping problem is exactly the same. It doesn't matter what type of stopping problem it is, how long it's been a problem or what kind of impact it's had on your life. There are no degrees, no types of problems that are more difficult than others. They're all a variation of the same wayward ego-based impulse to self-destruct. The only difference is how the impulse gets expressed.

Consider these familiar examples:

♥ Linda expresses her self-destructive impulse with food. She had a fight with her 14-year old son who said he hated her. She didn't think he really meant it, but it upset her more than she let on. While Linda was doing the grocery shopping, she picked up a few candy bars and ate them in the car to comfort herself.

♥ Mark expresses his self-destructive impulse with alcohol. He had another grinding day as a drone at work. When he got home his wife greeted him with her usual aloofness. He realizes she just isn't that into him and only goes through the motions of partnership. Mark gave himself a couple of martinis to numb out and keep doing what he has to do.

♥ Zack expresses his self-destructive impulse with marijuana. Zack is one of those people who can't seem to relax or talk to others without struggling for something to say. Before going out to a party, he smoked a joint to get mellow and to make it easier for him to open up.

♥ Joan expresses her self-destructive impulse with tobacco. As the owner of an upscale dress shop, she feels under pressure to always be thin and to always look good. Instead of snacking during the day or eating a full lunch, she goes out the back door of the store and smokes half a cigarette to keep herself on track. Joan knows cigarettes are unhealthy, but she thinks they're less objectionable than eating or getting fat.

Although it may seem tremendously important to you personally, your favored substance or habit doesn't really matter. Self-destruction is self-destruction. Any troublesome substance can easily be exchanged for another more socially acceptable, less attention-getting substance. Smoking for eating. Alcohol for prescription drugs. And so on. This is why people who quit smoking often turn to food and put on weight. *The substance or habit is simply a preference*, and one is not better, easier or less objectionable than another. Each one is a getting device that temporarily masks, distracts or provides relief from having a tense, unwanted feeling.

After all, who wants to feel tense? Sad? Unloved? Out of place? Or constantly pressured to be perfect? These are the yukky feelings we'd prefer to numb out or avoid. Of course, avoidance and sedation of unpleasant life energy is the core of the stopping problem, and we'll talk about this later on in the program. For the moment, acknowledge that you're trying to make yourself more comfortable or less emotionally pained. This effort comes from your profound goodness and is rooted in your profound goodness. Thank yourself. Appreciate yourself. You're doing the best with the tools you have on hand, but now you're ready for some improved tools that will work better for you.

A new tool kit is essential because the good feeling you get from the substance or behavior is only temporary and can't be relied on to provide more than brief relief. This is why it's the booby prize. Sure, it's easy to make trite platitudes about how worthy you are of having long-term relief, unshakeable happiness and true inner peace. Still, for most people, the booby prize has a strong appeal. It did for me. We're all tempted by the instant ability to numb out and feel good, even if it's just a little snippet of goodness. At least you get that snippet, and it's a sure thing. But there's a trade-off, and it's a big one. Ultimately the booby prize makes you feel worse, much worse, never better. And that bad feeling is a real killer, literally and figuratively.

So here you are, with the bright and hopeful idea that you'd prefer to live rather than continue to kill yourself. *The Power to Stop* is your life-saving program. You've been looking for a new and better way and this is it. More than anything else, the process of learning how to stop an unwanted habit is also the deeply calming practice of learning how to love yourself, accompanied by the extraordinary awareness of self as a holy, worthy, sacred being. Your new awareness will uplift your state of mind and renew your passion for life. How good is that?

Whatever age you are right now is the perfect age for stopping. It doesn't matter that you didn't stop yourself when you were younger or how long you've had the habit. Your gender doesn't matter. Your genetic predisposition doesn't matter. Your bank account doesn't matter. Your education level doesn't matter. Your support system (or lack of a support system) doesn't matter. Your physical condition doesn't matter. All that matters is your desire to stop. It brought you here, to *The Power to Stop*, and *The Power to Stop* will take you to a higher level of functionality and satisfaction.

Functionality is really important. Going through life without knowing how to stop yourself is like driving a car without knowing how to stop it. It's not practical. In fact, it's crazy. And it's harmful to yourself and others. So whether you're driving your car or driving through life, you need to be able to put on the brakes and stop. A crash, after all, is a harsh, inelegant and avoidable way to stop something. Yet, instead of stopping our unwanted habits, we continually let ourselves crash and burn.

Stopping is the opposite of going, just like putting on the brakes is the opposite of stepping on the gas. Stopping and going -- the skills are a pair, and both are essential. Both are needed to have a successful life. Both are available to us all, equally. It's the one way we're truly all the same. Our culture, however, puts overwhelming emphasis on action, which is going, and virtually no attention is put on inaction, which is stopping. This is too bad for all of us, because, as you are beginning to see, stopping is just as important as going. Maybe even more important.

When you don't know how to stop yourself, your life doesn't work. You don't feel good about yourself. Other people don't feel good about you either because your inability to stop self is most likely difficult to deal with. When you're really out-of-control and at risk of harming others, other people may try to force you to stop. This is what getting legally arrested is all about. The definition of arrest is *to bring to a stop*. Most people avoid the drama and distress of getting arrested, but eventually your own lifestyle draws attention to the value of stopping in ways that can't be ignored. Here are two real-life examples that show how stopping and an inability to stop produce a different life experience.

♥ *Martha and Jess*

Martha is home alone at night watching TV and gets the urge to eat something. In the kitchen, she finds a bag of Doritos, and returns to the couch to eat it. When she finishes the Doritos, she feels like eating something else, so she makes herself two pieces of toast with cream cheese and jelly. After that Martha finds a can of nuts and eats it. Then she has two bananas. Finally after finishing off the second banana, Martha stops eating. The next morning Martha wakes up feeling really bad. For one thing, she still feels bloated and she wishes she hadn't eaten all that food. But even worse, Martha feels like a big fat blob, and she hates herself for pigging out.

Jess is also home at night watching TV when she gets the urge to eat something. She had planned a regular evening snack for herself, and she goes and gets it. Jess eats her filling snack and enjoys it. She continues watching TV and then goes to bed. After waking up the next morning, Jess goes about her regular morning hygiene routine. She doesn't think about food, her evening snack or her body.

♥ *Larry and Eric*

Larry and Eric are work buddies. They have a big presentation to make the next day and decide to meet at a local bar after work to go over some last-minute details. Larry has a martini, and Eric has a soda. After the first martini, Larry has another one, and Eric has another soda. The men then finish up their talk. Eric goes home to eat and prepare for the next day. Larry spots a friend in the bar and stays to drink and hang out a while longer. He ends up staying until about 11:00. The next day Larry wakes up hung over, really hung over. He has a headache and an upset stomach, and he feels so sick he can't make it to the presentation. Larry calls Eric and apologizes for not being able to participate. He feels really, really bad about himself for letting Eric down, and worries about getting in trouble with his boss.

Eric starts the day full of energy and excitement about doing the presentation. On the one hand, he's very annoyed that Larry won't be there to do his part. Yet on the other hand, Eric is secretly pleased he'll be getting all the attention and credit. He starts thinking it's going to be a very good day.

Even though stopping is an essential and fundamental life skill, stopping or *not doing* isn't recognized or valued as a practical solution to life's problems. Most people, especially Americans, think that *doing something* or acting is the only way to get things done. This is an incomplete understanding of how the world works. Non-action gets things done, too.

The ingredients a chef leaves out of a recipe, for example, are just as important as the ingredients included in the recipe. An omelet wouldn't be an omelet if a gallon of paint and a bucket of dirt got added to the recipe. The colors, styles and pieces of furniture that a decorator leaves out of a room are just as important as the ones included in the room. An Asian-style room would be destroyed by adding early American furniture or Southwestern accent colors. What's left out or not done makes it possible for purpose, beauty, peace, and harmony to manifest. These are the qualities that are missing in a life that's dominated by any bad habit or crazy, unwanted behavior. Almost anything can be done the moment you want to do it. But doing everything and having everything doesn't translate into satisfaction and happiness. That's the cosmic joke of it all.

You've already tried the *doing* experiment. Now it's time to try the *not-doing* experiment. Here's the hard-core truth. Your unwanted habit will never stop tormenting you because it will never make you feel good about yourself. Not now. Not ever. No matter how much you try your best to *accept yourself* while you continue to engage in the bad habit, it won't work. Wasting yourself never works. Your bad habit will not run out of steam. It will not go away as you get older. You have to intend to stop it. You have to acquire the skills to stop it. And then you have to practice stopping over and over again until practicing disappears and stopping becomes a way of life.

The Power to Stop is dramatically different from every other habit-busting book available because it's disciplined, 30-day training program for learning four life-saving stopping skills. There's a skill for the mind, a skill for the spirit, a skill for the heart, and a skill for the body. Each skill by itself produces a result, but when all four are systematically combined into a daily program, the intention to stop magnifies and becomes a full life expression. Skill-building is progressive, where each day builds on the previous day. Nothing is ever asked that's too hard, and no super human effort is required.

In his book, *Zen Mind, Beginner's Mind*, author Shunryu Suzuki tells a story about the four different kinds of horses: excellent horses, good horses, poor horses, and bad horses. An excellent horse is very desirable because he'll do whatever the rider wants him to do just being asked. A good horse is also desirable because he'll do whatever is asked, but first needs to be inspired by seeing a whip. A poor horse is less desirable because he not only has to see the whip, he also has to feel it before he responds and does what the rider asks. And a bad horse is not desirable at all. A bad horse will only do what he's supposed to do after he's yelled at, whipped, and kicked with spurs. The bad horse has to get the message all the way to the marrow of his bones.

Everyone wants to be the best, most excellent horse, and no one wants to be the worst horse. But Suzuki helps us to understand how labels of goodness and badness are a paradox, which means that things are not always what they seem to be on the surface. The best horse is really the worst, least fortunate horse, and the worst horse is really the best, most fortunate horse. This is because the best horse isn't getting anything useful out of the situation. He's just robotically responding to a command and mindlessly going through life. The experience, therefore, has no value, no meaning. The worst horse, on the other hand, has the most to gain. He's forced to use the difficult situation to learn how to deliberately choose to act in another way. So even though it seems like bad luck, the worst horse is really having the best luck.

Your troublesome habit is also a paradox. What seems to be a disadvantage is actually an advantage because it's the perfect set up for profound personal growth, for the extraordinary accumulation of personal power and the remembrance of the self as love. Every troublesome habit or behavior is an expression of an abundance of energy. People with an abundance of energy always have the same hard time harnessing it and redirecting it in a more constructive way. The flip side of every worst horse troublesome behavior is always miracle work. *The Power to Stop* teaches you how to become a life safer or *savior*, and your ability to save naturally extends outward to others. Your miracle power is there, right now, waiting for you to notice it, claim it, use it.

Roseanne Barr, the comedian and actress once said, *"Nobody gives you power. You take it."* And that is what you are about to do. You are going to claim the power that you've forgotten. Power is your birthright. Many people mistakenly think that having power and courting power is a worldly rather than spiritual pursuit. And yes, of course, power is routinely used as a worldly commodity. People with political power win elections. People with financial power have the resources to buy more and finer things. People with sexual power attract more mates. Power makes life easier and more enjoyable, but power is not exclusively worldly. It's also desirable in the spiritual realm. People with spiritual power have the extra energy needed to end suffering and to perform miracles. When you are personally healed and whole, you will become an example of healing and a force for healing in our world.

The Power to Stop leads you to your power and to stopping success in ten observable, measurable ways:

1. *You will learn four life-saving stopping skills.*

   The Power to Stop teaches a set of four simple life-saving power skills that enable you to stop yourself. There's a power skill for the mind, which is setting an intention and holding it. There's a power skill for the spirit, which is reliance on inner peace to override the ego and tap into power. There's a power skill for the heart, which is making yourself happy and never sacrificing your happiness for any reason. And there's a power skill for the body, which is diffusing physical tension.

   No one else knows about these skills. No one else writes about these skills. No one else teaches them, and it's highly unlikely you'll stumble across the four steps by accident or by trial and error. These skills are unique and revolutionary, and they're only available at *The Power to Stop*.

2. *You will discover that stopping is a skill you can learn rather than a disease to be cured, psychological disorder to be corrected, or behavior to be modified.*

   The reason you don't know how to stop yourself is because you haven't yet learned how to stop yourself. Stopping is a skill the same as riding a bike or swimming or using a computer is a skill. But since stopping isn't recognized as a skill, it doesn't get taught in schools, families, churches or businesses. Where can you go to learn about stopping? There aren't a lot of choices. If your habit is moderate rather than extreme, AA won't appeal to you, and who can afford $20,000 a month or more for rehab? *The Power to Stop* gives you an easy way to learn stopping in the convenience and privacy of your own home. Contrary to popular belief, there's nothing woo-woo, repressive or alarming about stopping yourself. You will not be frustrated. You will not hurt yourself. You will not be unhappy.

3. *You will heal your body and your mind with the power of Love.*

    All healing is a direct result of love of self. You must be the one to provide the love because you are the one who is withholding it. No one else can do this for you, but you can be taught and inspired to do it for yourself. The best part about learning how to stop yourself is that you're also learning how to give yourself unshakeable, unconditional love. The kind you always dreamed about. How great is that?

    When the underlying feeling of self-love is present, there's no need to reach for excess food or a substance to feel good. This is why everything you do in *The Power to Stop* helps to bring the awareness of love to the forefront of your mind. Do you want to feel good about yourself or do you want the booby prize that substitutes for the good feeling?

4. *You will directly experience your Christ-self.*

    You will learn how to hold the awareness of your Christ-self for brief, regular moments. You do not need to become a fully enlightened being, someone who holds the awareness of the Christ-self all the time, to successfully stop yourself. All you need is an instant, one holy instant. The experience of self as sacred and holy adds meaning and underlying purpose to the stopping process. It transforms a routine, mechanical act into something that's mystical, miraculous and joyful. And most of all, it enables you to tap into power that defies gravity where all physical, earthly laws are temporarily suspended.

5. *You will recognize your wayward impulsive energy as vital life energy.*

The impulse to self-destruct appears in all of us. It's part of our human condition. Some of us, however, are more sensitive to it than others. You and I, for example, are those sensitive people. We feel it more deeply, and we respond to it more vigorously. Since the impulse never disappears, we have to figure out a constructive way to diffuse the impulse and deal with it without giving in and subtly killing ourselves. The four skills you learn in *The Power to Stop* work together to disrupt, neutralize and override the ever-present impulse to self-destruct.

6. *You will step into a fear-free zone.*

Break free from the fearful but immensely popular lies that hold you back. A lie, which is an idea, can be just as powerful as the truth, which is another idea, because both the lie and the truth produce a result. The difference between believing in a lie and believing in the truth is that one makes you happy and one doesn't. One sets you free, and the other binds you. *The Power to Stop* is radically committed to a wholly love-based, fearless ideology which is still rare on planet Earth. Fear is released by the refusal to buy into fearful ideas. This includes reversal of the fearful belief that disease is a cause rather than a result, the belief that full healing is not possible and recovery is never-ending, the belief in certain irreversible addictive traits and others.

7. *You will achieve spiritual fitness.*

Spiritual fitness and physical fitness are similar because they both rely on the principles of repetition and resistance to achieve a result. The goal of physical fitness is to develop physical strength and endurance. The goal of spiritual fitness is to develop spiritual strength and endurance to transcend the ego. Your unwanted habit is essential because it provides the much-needed resistance and a practical, daily reason for getting spiritually strong. Lighting candles and chanting phrases are lovely spiritual and religious practices, but transcendence of the ego is where and how you experience your Truth. *The Power to Stop* invites you to use the downward earthly pressure of the habit and to strategically *exploit* the stopping process as a fast, efficient, proven path to God.

8. *You won't waste time, energy on guilt or atoning for past mistakes.*

   Guilt is a trip to the dark side, where there is no light, no life, no growth. Some people think that a tiny bit of guilt is good for you, but it isn't. Guilt dramatically increases the impulse to self-destruct, and this is never good. Instead of diffusing tension, guilt increases it and makes it worse. There's no constructive use for guilt. None. Let the melodrama about your past go. Let the judgments about your personal badness go. So what if you made mistakes? Resist the temptation to *make up* for them, an unfortunate practice that takes the past and keeps it alive by dragging it into the present. The past does not exist, and the solution is not there. All attention needs to be focused on the present moment because this is the only place where power can be tapped and where stopping can occur.

9. *Your will hear, express and share the Voice for God.*

   The ego gives you the false message that you're weak, helpless and doomed. The Christ-self gives you the message that you're strong, powerful and the creator of your own life experience. Both messages are always available to you. You have to decide which one you want to receive and respond to. *The Power to Stop* teaches you how to choose the Voice for God by temporarily tuning into your Christ-self and temporarily tuning out the ego. The process of extracting, recording and sharing your own wise Voice is helpful because this how you come to believe in it, rely on it, and treat it as real.

10. *You will make yourself count.*

   The Power to Stop program is all about you. Your life counts. Your happiness counts. Your goals are important. Your life experience will be filled with meaning and value. Your own beauty, wholesomeness and courage will set your heart on fire. You are the only stopping case study that matters; none others are presented.

Stopping depends on not using your preferred substance, and there can be no compromise on this. This means no drinking, no using tobacco products, no drugging. Of course, in the case of out-of-control eating, it's not possible or desirable to abstain from food, but it is possible to abstain from sugar, high fructose corn syrup and highly processed carbohydrate foods made with fiberless flours. These are the substances that trigger and exacerbate out-of-control eating. (If you're an out-of-control eater, please refer to the addendum at the end of *The Power to Stop* for simple eating guidelines.)

The ability to tune out the ego and tap into power is blocked when substances of any kind, including excess food, dull the mind. This is why not using the substance is absolutely necessary. It's hard enough to hear the Voice for God as it is, and it's impossible when substances interfere with your thinking. Power is only available to a clear, sharp mind, not a dulled one. A sharp, clear mind has nothing to do with I.Q. and everything to do with taking life straight, without dilution.

You <u>can</u> take life straight. You <u>can</u> stop yourself. And <u>can</u> use your stopping experience to develop self-love, personal power and moments of enlightenment. The question is, will you? Every objection has been countered, and there's no reason left to procrastinate or delay. Make the decision now, my friend, to complete the whole 30-day *Power to Stop* program, no matter what. If it helps, you can think of me smiling at you and welcoming you.

When you're ready, slowly say this phrase out loud to yourself:

I intend to actively participate in the Power to Stop program for 30 days.

The Tibetans say you should never judge a situation because you never know when you're having good luck. You're having good luck right now, you just don't realize it yet.

FORMER CRAZY LADY TELLS ALL

Why I walk the talk for you

Remember that where your heart is, there is your treasure also.

A COURSE IN MIRACLES

Oh, yeah. I'm a former crazy lady, alright, and I'll get to that in a minute. First I want to tell you why I'm here for you. I am, you know, here for you. The recognition of my life mission to serve as your guide came to me, unexpectedly, on a trip to Scotland of all places! My husband and I are occasional world travelers. A few years ago we took a really wonderful and extensive coach tour through Great Britain, which includes England, Scotland and Wales. Our trip started in Edinburgh, the capital of Scotland, where I ate the requisite haggis, a much-hyped but wretched-tasting national specialty, made of sheep liver, heart and lungs. Ugh. It's highly doubtful I'll ever develop the taste for haggis.

Other Scottish delicacies were much easier for me to appreciate. Scotsmen in kilts, for example, were a constant visual treat. There's something about a man who's confident enough to wear a skirt that really gets your attention. And who can resist the lure of a lovely Scottish brogue? Words just sound better when they're spoken to you lyrically, like a song. Then there's the spectacular Scottish geography. Oh my goodness! The dramatic coast. The legendary highlands. The unspoiled lakes. Scotland is heaven for your eyes with one fantastic view after another.

As we were driving around sight-seeing, our tour director kept pointing out all the cairns along the way. Cairns are piles or stacks of rocks that point a direction. Today we have GPS technology and maps, but in earlier times, people relied on cairns to figure out whether to go right, left or straight. Cairns were simple enough for everyone to understand. Even people who couldn't read could quickly and accurately interpret a cairn.

Before going on this trip, I had never actually heard *cairn* pronounced before. In my head, whenever I read this word, I pronounced it cārn, with just one syllable. But our tour director pronounced it with two syllables, where the first syllable was pronounced like the word *care* and the second syllable was pronounced like the letter *n*. So when you put the two sounds together you get *care-n*, which is exactly the way you say my first name, Karen.

In that instant I somehow *knew* that my first name was also my purpose, and everything in me accepted this realization as truth. How cosmic is that? I, Karen, came to planet Earth to be a way pointer, a girl-guide, a Sherpa. Since I think of what I do as *walking the stopping mountain*, the image of a Sherpa, which is a type of guide most commonly associated with climbing Mount Everest in the Himalayas, particularly appeals to me. Up and down. Down and up. Year after year, a Sherpa climbs the mountain. He *knows* the mountain. He *knows* the weather conditions on the mountain. He *knows* what tools are needed on the mountains. He *knows* what clothes are needed on the mountain. Sherpa's serve humanity by showing other climbers what they know.

Sure, it's possible a climber might be able to make the trek without a Sherpa. But a Sherpa makes the climb safer. He makes it faster. He makes it more efficient. And above all, he makes it much more doable. Of course, climbers have to actually do the climb themselves. But the nimble Sherpa makes a difficult, sometimes treacherous and otherwise unlikely climb achievable, and this is exactly the kind of assistance I provide for you.

You and I are going to walk the stopping mountain together. By following in my footsteps, you'll learn how to make the same simple repetitive decisions that I make every day. These decisions will make it possible for you to stop yourself and to find meaning in the stopping process. I'll show you where to plant your feet, how to hold your heart, where to set your sights. You'll learn what mistakes to avoid and how to recover from mistakes when they crop up. It will be a grand adventure for us both. For now, I'm your humble servant and guide, but my goal is to give you the information, skills and inspiration to serve and guide yourself. That way you won't need to rely on me or on anyone else to stop yourself.

If I didn't walk the stopping mountain, I'd still be the same crazy lady who does crazy things and feels bad about herself. My great good fortune in life was to be born into a birth family where there was an abundance of ongoing drama and craziness. Life, after all, can be so dull without it. Most of the craziness was the common garden variety that we all experience: screaming, tiny acts of meanness, emotional torment, withdrawal of affection, not speaking. Normal stuff like that.

My mom was a first generation Italian, and her big, noisy, wonderful family taught me everything I know about old-style Italian feuds and vendettas. These were/are the kind of people who got mad and stayed mad for years, lifetimes even. One of my cousins, for example, absorbed a grievance held by his dad against my mom, and obligingly continued the feud into a second generation. Even now, after everyone is long dead, the grievance lives on. Carrying a grudge in support of a family member was the expected thing to do. *You're either with me or against me.* If I didn't automatically side with my Mom, she perceived it as the most heinous kind of betrayal, and I would distance myself from people I loved just to make her happy

Every grievance, whether real, imagined or exaggerated, was hashed out and relived around my mother's dining room table. This is where all the good stuff got revealed. My mother's five sisters and two brothers would all come over to our house, drink a whole lot, eat a whole lot, and tell all. Nothing was too secret to share. The conversation might be about husbands who wanted too much sex. Or children who got in trouble. Or money problems. Or my grand-father, who lived alone and was supported by his eight children, each one contributing $10 a month for his rent and food and then gossiping about who was late providing it. Who needs reality TV, when your life throbs with this kind of intensity, intimacy and tears? Oh my God, I loved it. Sometimes I physically ache to have the intimacy and connection I felt for my mom and her feisty five sisters back again. I can barely speak about it without tears coming to my eyes. Life around that dining room table was always exciting, sometimes painful and thoroughly over the edge.

It shouldn't surprise you, then, to discover that I became what I lived, an always exciting, sometimes full of pain, and often over-the-edge kind of person. My edginess, a/k/a craziness, was subtly encouraged and socially acceptable in every way. People always enjoy being entertained, and I for sure did my share of entertaining in a dark kind of way. Here's the catch. It would have all worked out pretty well, except that my craziness made me unhappy, sometimes seriously unhappy. Unhappiness and discomfort were my most predictable companions, but you would never know it by talking to me. Feelings like these were never shared with others. By the time I was a teenager I discovered that I could use food and alcohol for instant relief and for a moment of that comfort that I desperately wanted, and these quickly became my primary tools for dealing with everything I preferred to avoid. I loved the good feeling I got from pigging out or binge drinking. I adored relaxing in oblivion. I looked forward to every little bit of escape.

Many weekends were spent in an alcoholic glaze. I seem to remember I was into vodka and orange juice. For one thing, it didn't taste too much like alcohol, and for another, I could benignly disguise it as virgin juice. My family was distracted with bigger and better dramas, and rarely noticed I was buzzed or that I had a gazillion hangovers. They noticed my weight, though. I was always what you might call chunky, and a couple of times my weight spiraled up to over 200 pounds. This is what happens to you when you eat 6,000 or 7,000 calories a day for several consecutive months. My dirty little secret is that I'm one of those people who can eat a whole bag of bread (at once), a whole pumpkin pie (at once), and a whole bag of Oreo cookies (at once). You get the idea. My favorite food was whatever happened to be handy. I thought I was a bottomless pit, and I definitely believed I had a genetically-programmed, addictive personality. This genetic defect is something I lamented greatly and felt powerless to change.

Despite these challenges, my life more or less worked on many levels. I went to school. I held a job. I paid my bills. I looked normal. I said normal things. I did normal things. On another level, however, my life was very messy -- particularly my relationships. I knew how to complain and whine about my problems, but I didn't know how to resolve my problems. In fact, and I know this sounds preposterous, I didn't even realize that problems could be solved. I thought you just bucked up, made do and put up with intolerable situations. Really, that's what I thought, and that's what I did. All I had for dealing with my problems was my anger and my escape tools, and I used them. Thank God I wasn't completely without resources or I would have really been desperate!

That's who I was, but it's not who I am now. People who did not know me when I was younger find it hard to believe that I have a past littered with out-of-control behaviors because I now demonstrate unwavering discipline in many areas. My evolution from confused to certain, from angry to loving, and from powerless to powerful unfolded over a ten-year period in my forties and is still in process. It paralleled a dramatic increase in spiritual awareness and my personal dedication to a love-based way of life. Am I perfect? No. Do I live a perfect life? No. Do I completely avoid mistakes? No. But I'm as perfect as I need to be to provide a living example of what is possible.

You and I are exactly the same. We have a different version of the same story, that's all. This is why I'm certain we can both achieve the same result. As you now know, I didn't start out with discipline, inner strength and passionate purpose. Even though I was afraid, confused and unhappy, I was able to develop these positive, life-affirming qualities, and you can too. I didn't have a support group or an understanding coach to hold my hand and encourage me, but you will. I didn't have a process to follow, but you will. I didn't have much of anything except a glimmer of hope that there must be a better way to go through life than the way I was doing it. That tiny glimmer brought me to where I am today. It was enough. You have the same glimmer. Focus on it. Believe in it. It's telling you something important.

What is your glimmer of hope for yourself?

ON YOUR MARK

4 super simple start-up tasks

The only way to escape from misery is to recognize it and go the other way.

A COURSE IN MIRACLES

The Power to Stop requires very little advance preparation or additional cost. Please take care of these four easy start-up tasks before beginning the program.

1. Set up a binder or a manila folder and call it *My Miracle Stopping Journal.* Make the lettering and label as clear, neat and beautiful as you can make it. Be mindful of putting a copy of everything you create on your computer or by hand in your journal. Your journal will become the treasure chest of wisdom you extract from within yourself. Yes, I give you essential information, but your own wisdom is your most valuable asset. Give your own wisdom the top priority treatment it deserves.

2. Make sure you have a pair of thick-soled sneakers or walking shoes.

3. Get a timing device. A smart phone with a clock, a watch with a timer or a kitchen timer will do nicely.

4. You need access to a computer or to a device that enables you to visit www.powertostop.com. This is the place to get your stopping tools and to share/post your own stopping wisdom.

A pedometer is an optional but helpful tool. It's not necessary to have a pedometer to start the program, but consider picking one up along the way before you start the second week of the program. It's fun to track your daily steps.

Day 1

YOUR HEALING MIRACLE

Let it begin

> The miracle extends without your help, but you are
> needed that it can begin. Accept the miracle of healing.
>
> A COURSE IN MIRACLES

Everyone here on planet Earth feels the impulse to self-destruct in some way. Everyone! It comes from the ego, and it's part of our human condition. In heaven there is no ego and there is no impulse to self-destruct. Your unwanted behavior is an expression of the ego-based impulse to self-destruct, and undoing it is the mechanical device for transmuting your earthly experience into a more heavenly one. If you didn't have a so-called bad behavior, you'd have to develop one so that you could exploit it to get yourself on the fast track to heaven.

People who undo an unwanted behavior always have a spiritual awakening of some kind, whether its consciously recognized or not. This is because the undoing process automatically uplifts and aligns you with God. Awakening occurs regardless of the stopping methodology that's used. When the impulse to self-destruct is consistently overridden, the impulse stops luring you into its trap. It no longer has an effect, which means that nothing happens. There's no power. No more self-destruction. The impulse quietly disappears into the nothingness that it is.

You and I are challenged by *feeling* the pesky impulse to self-destruct more than the average person. We also *respond* to it more vigorously than the average person. The trick is to recognize your own sensitivity, but without investing any judgment or deep meaning into it. You're impulsive. So what! It doesn't have to mean something bad or unflattering. It doesn't have to be *interpreted* as a deep-rooted emotional problem or psychological dysfunction. In fact, it doesn't have to carry the stigma of a problem at all. This is because the flip side of self-destructive impulsiveness is miracle work. People with an abundance of impulsive energy have the biggest inherent potential for a spiritual awakening, and they have the biggest inherent potential to become the miracle workers of the world. That's you I'm talking about. You, a devoted and holy miracle worker in training.

Right now you feel the need to receive a miracle more than you feel the need to give one, and today's skill building exercises ask for the wholeness and healing miracle you deserve. Your healing drives everything we do together in *The Power to Stop* program. It's the single, unified purpose that binds and integrates every thought you're asked to hold, every action you're asked to perform, every word you're asked to read, every sentence you're asked to write. Each action gently and strategically leads you to your own wholeness and healing. It is, after all, healing that's wanted. The out-of-control behavior problem is not wanted. Everybody already knows that you get what you think about. The deck is stacked by thinking about what's wanted, which is your healing. Sure, there's some attention on the problem, but not much. Only what's minimally necessary.

Back to that pesky impulse, the miracle that's misfiring. Your new assignment is to figure out exactly what it is that you're feeling, buzzing around inside you. What would happen if you allow yourself to fully experience the physical sensation? How would you describe it? Is it a plane, a train or a speeding bullet? No, and it's not Superman either, but it *is* your super energy. Or more accurately, it's your super, mega-charged *life energy*. The sensations you feel in your body are your own life energy gone wild. Imagine that. Your life energy, which is normally imperceptible, is being expressed and experienced in a tangible way. This is what life without a filter feels like. It's possible to accept your lively impulse, get to know it, and make nice with it.

Of course, it's much easier to accept and work with life energy when it's peaceful and harmonious. Wild, intense and unruly life energy is scary and overwhelming. I liken it to being with a two-year old who's having a perpetual temper tantrum. No one really wants to deal with a screaming kid, and no one really wants to deal with wild, impulsive energy either. This is why it's so very tempting to sedate the impulse and make it go away as quickly as possible. Too bad this easy fix increases the momentum of your crazy energy and makes it stronger. Otherwise, it would be a great solution.

Have you ever seen the reality TV program with the English nanny who comes to the home of American parents who are being terrorized by their own children? The nanny calmly teaches the parents how to rescue themselves by dealing with their children rather than caving in to them. Dealing involves making and implementing a firm, consistent decision about what their children can and cannot do. A lot of times we see the parents resisting the nanny's advice, but ultimately, out of desperation, they finally break down and do what she asks. After all, as much as the parents might secretly want to run away, they can't. They're stuck, and there's no way but through. You can't run away from yourself either. You're stuck with your own life energy, and there's no way but through. You have to deal with yourself.

Once the parents get the hang of making a firm decision and saying and doing the same thing over and over and over again, the miracle happens. The kids respond. They calm down. They get easier to live with. They get easier to love. Once you get the hang of making a firm decision and saying and doing the same thing with yourself over and over and over again, your unruly impulsive energy responds. You calm down. You get easier to live with, and you begin to fall in love with yourself.

Energy always responds to decisive, unwaivering direction. Always. Unruly childish energy responds to firm and consistent adult direction, and unruly impulsive energy responds to firm and consistent adult direction. That's the rule, and you're not some kind of rare cosmic exception. You are afraid of yourself and your own life energy, but there's no reason to fear yourself or to avoid or apologize for who you are. Your life energy will follow your direction, but you have to do the boring and repetitious work of giving it direction.

Today you're going to look at your own wild impulsive energy, and calmly say *okay, this is what I have to work with*. Then you're going to start giving yourself conscious, strategic direction for taming your own energy, and then you're going to do the same thing, over and over, every day for the next 30 days. Your direction to self will be firm, but it will be not punitive or harsh. It will be consistent, but it will not be rushed. It will take effort, but it will not require more effort than necessary. One simple step after another, one day after another. This is how you discipline yourself, and discipline is not torment. Discipline is safety and structure, and you *do* need it.

If you watch the Nanny show, you'll see that no two-year old responds to a request the first time they hear it. Sometimes it takes five tries, sometimes it takes fifteen tries, sometimes it takes even more to get the kid to do what he or she is told. You might not respond the first time you direct yourself either. Overlook your initial resistance and non-response and keep giving yourself the same direction. Just because you don't respond the first time you ask yourself to do something new, doesn't mean anything. It doesn't mean you can't do it, and it doesn't mean you won't do it. Just keep asking. Your full mind, spirit, heart, body stopping intention becomes a command, an irresistible force that cannot be denied. When your purpose is so strong, failure is simply not an option. Keep your promise to complete the full 30-days, no matter what.

Whether you recognize it or not, your wayward life energy is your most precious asset. Ask a person with a terminal illness or a prisoner on death row, and they'll tell you this is so. Your valuable life energy can be captured and redeployed to miracle work. For me, personally, thinking of myself as a miracle worker sets my heart on fire a little bit. Okay, a lot. It gives me a purpose, and this purpose enables me to perceive my bodily sensations as useful, tolerable and sometimes even beautiful.

All this comes from a change of mind *ahead of time* about what my life energy is to be used for.

—— ✦ ——

DAY 1 STOPPING PRACTICE

Write down all your stopping practice responses in your *Miracle Stopping Journal*. Note whether you completed, partially completed or didn't perform the activities. Don't hide anything from yourself. Follow this protocol every day.

MIND: The skill of the mind is to make a decision and hold it.

1. Make the intention to heal yourself and to break free of your unwanted behavior. For now, use this format for expressing your intention.

    I break free of _____ (whatever it is you want to stop) by healing myself with deep inner peace and self-love.

2. Write your intention in long-hand three times in your *Miracle Stopping Journal*. Make your writing as beautiful and legible as you can.

3. Say your intention out loud, slowly and calmly, three times.

4. Sometime during the day, allow yourself to fully notice and experience your craving for whatever it is you want. Then do your best to describe your physical experience.

    •   When does it come to you? What time of day is it? Is it always the same?

    •   Try to observe what comes first: a physical sensation or a thought?

    •   What are you thinking while you're having the experience?

    •   How does it feel? Where in your body do you have the experience? What is the sensation?

    •   How long does it last?

SPIRIT: The skill of the spirit is to experience an instant of inner peace so that you can turn off the ego and connect with your Christ-self.

For the time being, please put aside any other meditation or mind-training techniques you may have practiced in the past, and for the next 30 days use the technique I give you. Every day I'll provide a short meditation phrase, which you'll slowly repeat over and over in your mind for the prescribed amount of time. It's easy to learn and do.

Today's meditation phrase

I am entitled to a healing miracle. I want a healing miracle. I expect a healing miracle.

Sit in a comfortable private place and repeat today's phrase for a full three minutes. (Use your timing device.) More time is okay if it's not a strain and feels comfortable to you. When you're done, sit in stillness for another 30 seconds.

HEART: The skill of the heart is to make self happy. Your happiness is the most important thing in the world and cannot be sacrificed for any reason.

Describe your healing miracle. What makes you happy about the prospect of being healed?

BODY: The skill of the body is to use physical tension to diffuse physical tension.

You'll be doing a brief period of consecutive physical activity six days out of every seven. Activities include aerobic exercise, strength training and stretching. It's assumed that you're <u>not</u> used to regular exercise and that you're out of shape. This is why the first week is a very gentle, very easy introduction to physical conditioning where you're not asked to do more 10 minutes of activity at any one time. If, however, you already engage in regular physical activity, you can substitute your own routine and time parameters. Do your best to include all three types of activities into your weekly exercise regime.

Here's an overview of your activity schedule for week one:

Day 1	Day 2	Day 3	Day 4	Day 5	Day 6	Day 7
Aerobic	Strength	Aerobic	Strength	Aerobic	Flexibility	Off

Today's activity

Type Exercise: Aerobics

Activity: <u>Brisk</u> walking

Time: 10 <u>continuous</u> minutes

(more time is okay, but don't burn yourself out).

Write about your exercise experience. When did you do it, where did you do it, how did it feel.

Day 2
WHAT'S LOVE GOT TO DO WITH IT
Be the love you seek

If you achieve the faintest glimmer of what love means today, you have advanced in distance without measure and in time beyond the count of years.

A COURSE IN MIRACLES

The problem with the word *love* is that it means different things to different people, and this creates a real puzzle. Whose definition, for example, do you accept and whose definition do you live by? Every time I do a *Power to Stop* get extreme results boot camp or seminar, I always include a group activity where everyone gives a one word definition of love. Depending on the amount of people in the room, I might end up with 20 to 40 beautiful but different words that mean love. Asking yourself to remember so many qualities isn't practical, and it's certainly not possible to live them all either.

Then there's the whole social component to consider. Does *love* mean being in special relationship with someone? Is it marriage? Children? Sexual chemistry? How many look for a physical charge before they extend love to another? Religions have a big influence on our ideas about love, too. They tend to mix the idea of love with the idea of sacrifice, which gets us all messed up. In fact, God and sacrifice is such a big topic and such a major block to love that I devote a whole lesson to it, which we'll talk about on another day. In the meantime, you might be tempted to think you have to suffer, sacrifice, kill or be killed to demonstrate your love and worthiness to God. Even the love masters, the best-selling religious and secular people who make a living talking about love and writing about love don't have a common, universal definition for us. If they can't agree, who can? Are you beginning to see how all these layers upon layers of meaning get piled onto the word *love* and this gets us hopelessly confused and overburdened with the difficulty of being all things to all people under all conditions.

Then there's the fact that sometimes our most well-intended personal definitions of love get us on the wrong track. Here's what I mean. Everyone agrees that love is kind, but every now and then being kind to another person results in unkindness to self or a sacrifice of self. So even though you make another person feel good with your kindness, you end up feeling bad about yourself. Is this really love? See how tricky it gets? See how scary it can be? What if love really is personal sacrifice? Do you want to embrace something that's so much work or that might involve pain or loss of face? This is why for now, for the next 29 days we have together, we're going to give up the futile attempt to contain love in a convenient little box or to define it with limiting words. We can't do it. Love is too big. It's too mysterious, too abstract, too expansive, too sacred. Love simply cannot be contained. So instead of knocking our heads against the wall and attempting the impossible, we're going to take a completely different tack. We cannot agree on what love is, but we can at least agree and recognize love by what it isn't, and here it is: love is not attack. Or said another way, love is harmless. If you're not attacking yourself or another, you're acting in love. It really is that simple and uncomplicated.

Refraining from attack is a monumental act of love, but it's not recognized as an act of love. That's the hard part, isn't it? You don't get any points for refraining from attack. It doesn't draw attention to you. There's no emotional high. Of course it's nice to hear and say the *I love you* words, but love doesn't depend on words. It doesn't depend on gifts or vows or service or any other condition, either. The one and only condition that Love requires is the conscious, deliberate *holding back* or refraining from attack. How elegant. How simple. How powerful. And most importantly, how obvious! You don't need to carry around a crib sheet of reminders. You don't need to go to an advisor for analysis or interpretation. You can always reflect and figure it out on your own. Are you attacking yourself or another or not? Are you acting harmlessly or not? That's all you need to know. Ever.

A fundamental attack thought that isn't recognized as an attack thought is the concept of specialness. Specialness is the idea that you can get exclusive and better love for yourself by being separate, unique and distinguished in some way. Everyone in every culture believes that love is special. It's the one true religion, the one idol we all worship. When specialness isn't honored, we feel justified in attacking ourselves with sadness or in attacking others with anger. Parents are supposed to tell us we're unique and special. If they don't, we feel short-changed and entitled to hate them. Spouses are supposed to treat us in a special way. If they don't, we feel betrayed and entitled to hate them. Educators are supposed to tell us we're special. If they're lax about this, we feel deprived of self-esteem and entitled to hate them. Employers are supposed to tell us we're special. If they don't appreciate our unique contributions, we say bad things and feel entitled to hate them. Whenever special attention is withheld or withdrawn, hatefulness towards self and others is justified.

Even religions get into the specialness act. They tell us God thinks we're special, and who doesn't believe it? God created us, so we're *supposed* to be unique and special to Him. We think we're so important, we imagine that God is vigilantly watching our every move, like Santa, but without the presents. It's heresy to suggest that God doesn't watch us, or that His love isn't special, but He doesn't and it isn't. God's love is completely, utterly ordinary and without any distinction. His love shines on everyone, endlessly and eternally. It's called immutable because God's love can't be altered or influenced by people, behaviors, events or things. He doesn't have to watch us because His love is for free, without any conditions or taboos attached to it. Nothing can turn God's love off. Nothing can change it in anyway. You could be the worst screw up in the world, and it wouldn't change God's love for you. You could be the most holy, devout person and it wouldn't change God's love for you. There is no extra kudo from God for making a huge donation to your church. In fact, there's nothing you can do to draw more attention and love to yourself. God's world is not special. The magical spell of specialness only exists here, in the ego's word, which is in your mind.

As you already know, the ego and the Christ-self both share the mind, but in the untrained mind ego thoughts dominate. Typically, there's very little deliberate interaction with the Christ-self. This means *your thoughts automatically default to self-destructive ego thoughts.* Hateful thoughts that come from your own mind are embraced and believed. You think your hateful thought is real and important, and this gets you all riled up and feeling bad. Ego feeds on the unsettling feelings and the intense emotions these yukky thoughts generate. The more you indulge your feelings of anxiety, guilt, anger or despair, the stronger the ego gets, and the more you experience the urge to self-destruct. Thoughts, beliefs and emotional reactions churn round and round and create the same pattern of self-destructive existence over and over again. Buddhists have a word for this endless cycle of suffering. They call it *samsara*, and the only way to break free is by breaking the pattern, which is what you're doing.

The uncomfortable attack thoughts you hold in your mind result in uncomfortable sensations you experience *through* your body. Or said another way, your hateful and destructive thoughts are physically expressed as the impulse to self-destruct. Thought produces form, which in this case is the impulse. The physical impulse doesn't produce your hateful thought. See how it works? It seems like your body is in control, but it's not. This is what makes the body such an ideal learning device. Attack thoughts are relatively easy to ignore or to judge as not so bad, but your body is right there in your face with all its aches and dysfunctions and urgings. Hard to ignore that!

Even though the body and its senses are in the domain of the ego, the body is basically a neutral object and it willingly serves whatever part of the mind that dominates. For now the ego is in control, and the body is its slave. The good news is you have the power to use your Christ-mind to reinterpret the purpose of your body and the body's sensory data if you want to. Your Christ-self will always lead you away from focus on the body and towards focus on the Christ-mind. There are no bodies in heaven, but this is not a reason to hate the body or to disregard it. The Christ that dwells within loves your body.

Like most people, you probably believe in the wisdom of the body. It's the conviction that your body is trying to communicate some kind of intelligence to you through sensations in your body. Sure, you're getting messages. But they're not from your body, which has no intelligence. They're from your ego mind which dominates your body and communicates to you through its senses and sensations. Why pay attention to messages that come from an ego that is not your friend? What good is a message that leads you down an uncreative, weak and helpless path? The body can only express wisdom when it's under conscious and creative control of the Christ-mind, and yours is clearly not. At least not yet.

For now, consider the possibility that harmless, peaceful thoughts in your mind result in harmless, peaceful sensations in your body. This is why we devote so much time and energy on calming down, diffusing tension and training your mind to focus on loving and benign thoughts.

DAY 2 STOPPING PRACTICE

MIND: The skill of the mind is to make a decision and hold it.

1. Write your intention to stop three times in long-hand. Make your writing an act of love. How neat, beautiful and legible can you do it?

2. Say your intention out loud, slowly, three times.

3. Answer this question: What's the single most important reason for stopping yourself? Write down your answer in your *Miracle Stopping Journal*.

SPIRIT: The skill of the spirit is to experience inner peace so that you can temporarily turn off the ego and connect with your Christ-self.

Sit in a comfortable position in a private place. Repeat the phrase over and over in your mind, slowly, for a full five minutes. Then sit in stillness for another 60 seconds. More time is okay if it feels right to you and if it's not a strain.

Today's meditation phrase

I will not hurt myself again today.

Say the phrase *I will not hurt myself again today* at least 3 more times during the day. Before you eat lunch, before you eat dinner, and before you go to bed at night is ideal.

HEART: The skill of the heart is to make self happy. Your happiness is the most important thing in the world and cannot be sacrificed for any reason.

Write about one moment in your day today that you most enjoyed. What exactly were you doing? Were you active or passive? Were you alone or in company with others? How long did the moment last? How did you recognize your own happiness?

Express your gratitude to yourself for this moment of happiness. Express awareness that your own happiness is possible. How can you extend your feeling of happiness one minute longer?

BODY: The skill of the body is to use physical tension to diffuse physical tension.

If needed, go to www.powertostop.com/tools for a short and easy exercise routine or for video instruction.

Type Exercise:	Strength Training
Activity:	Core conditioning/abdominal exercise
Time:	6-10 minutes

Write about your exercise experience: when you did it, where you did it, how long you did it and how it felt.

Day 3

SAVING YOURSELF IS LITERAL

Hold, contain and conserve the energy in your impulse

You will learn salvation because you will learn how to save.

A COURSE IN MIRACLES

Can you believe Jimmy Buffet wrote *Margaritaville* over 30 years ago, back in 1977? As a drinking anthem, it's still as popular today as it was then. Maybe even more popular because Buffet's Margaritaville empire of restaurants and products keeps growing and growing. Everyone who's ever hung out in a bar in a warm weather vacation destination knows the *wasting away again in Margaritaville* chorus and merrily sings along.

*Wasted i*s a hip term for getting drunk or out-of-it on alcohol or drugs. It's supposed to be a figurative term, but wasting isn't figurative at all. It's literal. Little by little your life energy dribbles and drains away. You have a vague feeling that something isn't quite right, but you can't put your finger on it. You don't really care one way or another what happens. There's a drab quality to your life. It's a big whatever. Nothing sparkles any more. This is wasting. It's a slow, persistent, subtle, barely perceptible leakage of life that robs you of your vitality and turns you into a shuffling, nearly-dead zombie.

Interestingly, the word *devil* is derived from the Greek word *diabolical*, which means good for nothing. Wasting, of course, is good for nothing. When you waste your life energy on something that has no value or purpose, you're acting diabolically. Diabolical actions always make you feel bad about yourself. The bad feeling is usually interpreted as a moral judgment or an unsavory psychological condition of some kind, but it's not. The bad feeling is the tangible, literal experience of wasting away.

Society uses a hierarchical degree system that judges and categorizes wasting based on the severity of the life wasting experience. Depending on where it falls on the scale, wasting is either embraced, tolerated or punished. *Mild* wasting isn't just okay, it's desirable because light sedation relaxes you and takes the edge off. *Moderate* wasting is usually acceptable, but judgment about badness and wrongness starts creeping in. *Severe* wasting is clearly perceived as self-destructive and wrong. When there is no doubt, no ambiguity, we come out with our full artillery and judge these behaviors as something that must be stopped, rehabbed, medicated, changed, helped, punished or put out of sight. Otherwise, no one really cares one way or another whether you waste yourself or not.

Look at your own thoughts about light social drinking, weekend drugging, infrequent smoking or occasionally pigging out. Like most people, you probably perceive a light degree of waste as pleasurable, sometimes beneficial, and definitely okay. Now look at your views about a moderate degree of over drinking, drugging, eating or sexing. The situation might be less than ideal, but if the person's life is more or less functional, it's still okay. Now look at your own perception about extreme wasting. It's bad, right? No question.

See how your opinion of wasting gets confused and complicated? Degrees blur the line and make it difficult to figure out what you're doing with your own life energy. Should you buy into the prevalent social opinion, which says go ahead and kill yourself a little? It's a real challenge because you will not get clear, unambiguous, uncompromising direction from our ego-based world. Every expert has a different opinion. Every study has a different result. All you will ever hear is contradiction, confusion and conflict. This is why it's essential to understand the difference between killing yourself and not killing yourself. Then you can correct your core belief about wasting, and go your own way.

So now you know that life energy can be wasted, but did you also know that it can be saved? Saving your life energy works exactly the same as saving your money. Money is saved by not using it. Likewise, life energy is saved by not using it. The energy to be saved is right there inside the habit, behavior or compulsion that's troubling you. Instead of wasting your own wild but precious energy, you accept it and keep it. *Keeping* or *holding* is the mechanical way that saving occurs. When you make a money deposit, the bank accepts and keeps your money. To make a life energy deposit, you accept and keep your life energy instead of throwing it away.

The saving process is also an accumulation process. Saved money accumulates. Saved life energy accumulates, too. When you regularly deposit money in your bank account, your supply of money compounds and grows. When you regularly make energy deposits into your life energy account, your supply of life energy also compounds and grows. Eventually a vast, invisible savings account of life energy develops. This is commonly known as personal power or inner strength. Personal power and inner strength can be used on a practical level to do whatever you want with your life and to make it work better. It can be used on a spiritual level as a conduit for miracles. You will need this savings account of energy to live without the structure and automation provided by the ego.

The saving of life energy can also viewed from a big-picture strategic perspective as a conservation practice. Conservation is a fancy word for *not using* a resource even though it happens to be available. It's about making the smallest energy impact or leaving the smallest energy consumption foot print. Conservation of land is the practice of leaving land undeveloped. Conservation of fuel is the practice of using less gas or coal or electricity. Conservation of money is the practice of cutting out unnecessary expenses. Conservation of life energy is about the practice of cutting out the thoughts, emotions and acts that aren't essential or life-affirming. Conservation is an important practical survival strategy, and it's an important spiritual survival strategy.

There's a PBS documentary floating around about how the herds of bison in Yellowstone National Park successfully deal with harsh winter conditions by conserving their energy. The bison are photographed toughing out harsh storm conditions by herding together to conserve body heat. People don't herd the bison together. They do it themselves, naturally. The bison instinctively know they can conserve energy by standing perfectly still in the herd. Hordes of PBS photographers and staff people are within sight, but the bison don't waste any energy looking at them. They don't move their heads. They don't make any noise. They don't even blink their eyes. Bison *know* their survival depends on total peace and stillness. The same energy conservation phenomena can be observed in dogs in poverty stricken nations. My husband and I have had the life-changing privilege of traveling around the world. I can tell you from firsthand experience that wherever you see extreme poverty, you also see emaciated dogs. Thousands of them. These dogs don't waste any energy wagging their tails, jumping up and down to greet you, or doing cute doggie tricks. The dogs are perfectly still. They don't care what you say or do. They don't care if you have money. The dogs need every iota of energy to survive the next minute, the next day, the next month.

Your salvation depends on the conservation of your own energy. Conservation techniques include moments of inner peace, guidance from within for efficient and right direction, and calming self down so that energy isn't expended on emotional turmoil and upset. All of these techniques work together to achieve the same goal of saving self by *containing* or *not using* the energy that resides in your unwanted habits and impulses. Salvation is the ordinary practical experience of saving your life energy. It's not an abstract concept that only happens when you say you believe in a deity or pray in a church. Only you can save yourself because only you can make the decision to save or waste your precious life energy. No one can do the work of saving you except you.

DAY 3 STOPPING PRACTICE

MIND: The skill of the mind is to make a decision and hold it.

1. Refine your intention statement by adding two or three descriptive words that make it come more alive and inspiring to you. Two examples are provided below, but use your own words so that your intention is charged with personal meaning.

   Example #1: eagerness and confidence

   I <u>eagerly</u> and <u>confidently</u> break free of _____ (the unwanted behavior) by using deep inner peace and self-love to heal myself.

   Example #2: relaxation and satisfaction
   Peace <u>relaxes</u> me and <u>fills me up</u>. My own stillness undoes _____ (the unwanted behavior) and heals me in every way.

2. Write your new intention in long-hand five times. Make your writing an act of love and fully conscious purpose.

3. Say your intention out loud five times, slowly.

4. Briefly describe what stopping looks like when it manifests in your life. Use any of these questions to prompt your thinking.

   - What does your face look like as you stop yourself?

   - What are your hands doing?

   - What position is your body in?

   - Where are you?

   - What time of day is it?

   - Who are you with, if anyone?

   - What does it feel like?

   - How long does it take?

SPIRIT: The skill of the spirit is to experience an instant of inner peace so that you can turn off the ego and connect with your Christ-self.

Today's practice period is one 7-minute meditation period. Sit in a comfortable private place, shut your eyes and slowly repeat today's phrase for the designated time. Then sit in stillness for another 30-60 seconds, or longer, if it feels comfortable to you.

Today's meditation phrase

My salvation comes from me.

HEART: The skill of the heart is to make self happy. Your happiness is the most important thing in the world and cannot be sacrificed for any reason.

Answer these three questions

1. I want to stop myself, but I scare myself by imagining
   _____*(what is your most fearful idea about stopping)*

2. I intend to stop myself, and I uplift myself by imagining
   _____*(what is your highest vision of stopping yourself)*

3. Briefly explain why your highest vision is actually possible.

BODY: The skill of the body is to use physical tension to diffuse physical tension.

Type Exercise: Aerobic

Activity: <u>Brisk</u> walking

Time: 10 <u>continuous</u> minutes (more is okay)

Write about your exercise experience. When did you do it? Where did you do it? How long did you do it? How did it feel?

Day 4

POWER, BABY, POWER

Stop going to the dark side

Heaven is chosen consciously. The choice cannot be made
until alternatives are accurately seen and understood.

A COURSE IN MIRACLES

Power makes the world go round. People with physical power have more strength and endurance. People with financial power buy more things. People with political power rule the world. People with sexual power attract more mates. People with social power have more friends. People with spiritual power end suffering and do miracles. Everybody wants some kind of power. You, for example, want stopping power. Power seems to be mysterious because you can't see it or touch it directly. You can only see it indirectly through the result. Technically, power is a tangible result produced from an intangible force. This intangible force is your desire, and it's the most dominant force in your life because it delivers everything you see, feel or experience. The more you want something, the more formidable your force. So we can say that everyone is a powerful being because everyone wants something, and everyone is able to produce a result of some kind.

The most common misperception about power is that it's not godly or wholesome. Denial of desire and the powerful results that come from desire leads to inner conflict and confusion. It also creates the false idea that it's more desirable to be powerless or weak. *Maybe God wants us to suppress our desire for things or experiences or relationships we want to have.* It's like trying to go forward with the brakes on. You never allow yourself to feel good about wanting something or having something. There's no spiritual or earthly advantage for denying your own strength or in refusing to cultivate strength.

Power only gets problematic when harm is introduced into the equation. Some desires are harmful, and this is the best reason for going within to ask for guidance about whether or not you should act on them. The desire to act on your desire to over eat, drink, drug or smoke falls into this category. Another problem with power crops up when harmful methods are used to get what's wanted. I call this *going to the dark side.* The easiest thing in the world is to want something so badly that you *do whatever it takes* to get it. *Doing whatever it takes* inevitably leads to attack on yourself or others. Attack is the world's most preferred *getting* device. It's quick, it's simple, it takes no training, and it has about a 99.999% success rate. Even 2-year olds can do it. It's the old idea that the end justifies the means. Or said another way, as long as you get what you want, it doesn't matter *how* you get it. Who cares about being love when what you want is hanging out there at risk of not being fulfilled?

People who aren't aware that love is harmless routinely go to the dark side to get what's wanted. For most folks, physically forcing someone to do your will is pretty extreme and socially taboo, but it's still done. That said, other means are much more likely, and they're just as effective. Consider how many times you've complained to get your way. What about exaggerating, whining or begging to force others into doing your wishes? Outright lying works pretty well if you don't do it too often. Then there are threats, pitching fits and being a drama queen or king. And who can forget that perennial favorite, the guilt trip? In the unlikely event that all these popular *getting* devices fail, you can always rely on the favorite technique of all moms everywhere, bribing.

Even praying to God involves the predictable trip to the dark side. It doesn't matter which God you believe in or what religion you prefer, everyone universally thinks you can do something special to *get* God's favor. We're all intimately familiar with the world famous God-bargain. It's the one that goes *I'll do this for you, if you do that for me.* We've all played around with sacrifice, too. Have you ever given up something you loved, at least for a little while, to win points with God? Do you ever make a big donation to your church and expect a big reward here on earth or in heaven? How about begging and pleading? And what about supplicating yourself? Does it really work to remind God about what a miserable sinner you are? All of these God-practices, however lovely or not-so-lovely, are a way of saying *I'm not worthy of getting what I want just because I want it, so I have to do something extra to become more worthy.*

Whenever you go to the dark side and use attack to get something you want, you're reinforcing the same dreary, dismal message. *I'm not good enough. I'm not worthy enough. I'm not lovable enough. I'm not powerful enough. Consequently, I have to do something to compensate for my shortcoming and coerce God and everyone else to please me.* Who wouldn't use food, alcohol or drugs to drown out this desperate message? No one likes to dwell on the dark side or to admit that darkness is their preferred life-coping strategy. We'd rather talk about living in light and shining our light and doing woo-woo spiritual things or performing religious rituals. Then the ordinary opportunity to get something you want pops up, like it does every single day of your life, and you go right to the dark side to get it.

Face it. The people in your immediate world don't want to put up with your antics. They don't want to suffer from your emotional torment, threats or bad moods. This is why they usually do what it takes to shut you up or to at least turn down your melodrama. All things considered, darkness is tremendously effective. Why bother to shine your light when shining your dark gets the job done? Consequently, there's no reason, no inspiration to learn about the love-based experience of power when you have dark power so handily at your disposal.

You can, of course, continue to go to the dark side as long as you want, but it will block you from experiencing yourself as a loving, worthy and enlightened being. Our goal today is to cut through this block and instill the desire for worthiness and the experience of self as Love. The tool for having the experience of worthiness and for living in light is *asking for what you want.* Isn't it amazing that you can simply ask for what you want and get it? Asking for something isn't always the fastest or easiest way to get something, but it makes you feel better about yourself.

The one prerequisite of asking for what you want is knowing what you want. This is another one of those things that sounds ridiculously simple, but isn't. If you don't take the time to get clear about the specific result you want, you automatically default to what the ego wants, which is vengeance. You know the ego is in control when you start complaining about what's not wanted. The first, middle and last rule of asking is to *ask only for what's wanted*. All the other ka-ka gets left out. Ka-ka is stuff like using threatening and angry voice tones, complaining, name-calling, forcing, guilt trips, bribes or some other harmful contrivance. It takes real awareness to *not say* the ka-ka, but this is your task at hand. Not saying harmful garbage is a way of experiencing yourself as love and cleaning up your worthiness act. This doesn't mean you can't disagree or that you can't want to correct a problem. It means that you can't disagree or correct problems with harmful language or other behaviors. When you don't put the garbage into your communications, you never have to go back and pick up after yourself. There's no trash. No dead bodies. No angst. Less drama. There's always the possibility that plainly speaking your request to others *might* result in someone else feeling bad. We are, of course, dealing with egos. But it's much less likely.

Here are two examples of how to ask for something. The first example is how to ask in darkness. The second example is how to ask in light. Both involve the same situation. A wife is unhappy because her husband leaves the toilet seat up after he pees. The wife wants her husband to remember to put the toilet seat up.

Example #1: Asking in darkness

I can't believe you left the toilet seat up again. It's disgusting for me to have to deal with this, and it's demeaning to women in general. What's wrong with you? Are you intentionally being rude or is it just your nature to be annoying? Don't expect any favors from me until you get this problem solved. How many times do I have to bring this up? I'm starting to think you're very stupid.

Example #2: Asking in light

Honey, I would really appreciate it if you'd remember to put the toilet seat up. I know it's a small thing to you, but it's a big thing to me.

Treat your request like a prayer. This will automatically remind you to use voice tones and words that are gentle rather than harsh. It will automatically remind you that no matter who you're talking to, whether it's your lover, your child, your employer, your server in a restaurant, or the person who answers the phone from India, that this person is worthy of your love-based request. When you give worthiness, you automatically receive it. Prayer is often used as a way of asking God for something and having faith it will be answered. Asking is a way of requesting something and having faith it will be answered. There is no difference.

Starting today, bring your awareness to your own reliance on darkness to get what you want in life. Don't be afraid to objectively look at how you express yourself. What voice quality comes out? What words come out? What dark technique (or set of techniques) comes out? Awareness is all that's required. That means no judgment and no guilt. Fussing about past trips to the dark side is not allowed. Experiment with making simple, unencumbered requests as they come up. This one simple technique, if used consistently, will begin to restore your sense of goodness, worthiness and power.

DAY 4 STOPPING PRACTICE

MIND: The skill of the mind is to make a decision and hold it.

1. Read your intention statement and write it in long-hand, slowly, five times. Concentrate on each word as you write it. Make the act of writing an act of love. As always, do your best to make your handwriting as neat, legible and beautiful as possible.

2. Say your intention out loud five times, slowly.

3. Observe yourself throughout the day. Then write about your favorite *dark side* technique. Take care not to apologize for yourself or judge yourself.

4. Who is the most powerful person you personally know? What characteristics make this person powerful in your eyes?

SPIRIT: The skill of the spirit is to experience an instant of inner peace so that you can turn off the ego and connect with your Christ-self.

Sit in a comfortable private place and slowly repeat today's phrase for one 7-minute period. Then sit in stillness for another 60 seconds or longer if it feels comfortable to you. Say the phrase at least 3 more times throughout the day. Before lunch, before dinner and before going to bed at night is ideal.

Today's meditation phrase

I trust my brothers and sisters who are one with me.

HEART: The skill of the heart is to make self happy. Your happiness is the most important thing in the world and cannot be sacrificed for any reason.

Answer these questions:

1. Briefly write about one real life experience (it can be at any age), where you trusted yourself, wholly and completely.

2. Explain why trust of others is essential for the experience of power that comes from love.

3. Why does trusting make you happy?

BODY: The skill of the body is to use physical tension to diffuse physical tension.

If needed, go to www.powertostop.com/tools for a short and easy exercise routine or for video instruction.

Type Exercise:	Strength Training
Activity:	Lower body
Time:	10 minutes

Write about your exercise experience: When, where, how-long, how you feel.

Day 5

STOPPING HAPPENS IN THE PRESENT MOMENT

Your past does not exist

How can you who are so holy suffer? All your past except
its beauty is gone, and nothing is left but a blessing.

A COURSE IN MIRACLES

TLC's *What Not to Wear* is a program about fixing clothing mistakes. Hosts Stacy London and Clinton Kelly are upbeat, savvy fashionistas who always find practical, beautiful clothing solutions for the featured bad dresser of the week. I especially appreciate the non-judgmental way Stacy and Clinton do their work. They always accept the person, *as is,* without making a big deal about why or how he/she got in such bad fashion shape. Stacy and Clinton teach the TV client how to work with his/her body shape and physical features to dress better and to present him or herself better. If the TV client is overweight, for example, Stacy and Clinton help the person to choose clothes that fit appropriately and that look good regardless of weight. If the person is a stay at-home-mom, they show her how to choose clothes that reflect that lifestyle. If the person likes to dress in a way that's dramatic and attention-getting, they incorporate drama into the fashion solution without going over the top.

Part of the fashion renovation process always involves going through the TV client's current wardrobe and ruthlessly throwing out everything that doesn't work. People resist this clearing out process and get in a big huff when Stacy and Clinton suggest a piece has gotta go even if the item doesn't fit, doesn't look particularly attractive and doesn't match with anything. Stacy and Clinton never, ever try to fix clothing mistakes or find a reason to keep them. Instead, all mistakes are tossed out. This forces the TV client to make new choices and to start fresh instead of continuing to rely on past dressing mistakes while going forward.

The big surprise is that once the TV client finally <u>gets rid of his or her dressing mistakes</u> and learns how to solve his or her dressing and self-presentation problem, a lot of other problems get solved along with it. Enthusiasm for life returns. Confidence returns. Smiling returns. A willingness to go out, be social and connect with others returns. It's important to recall that nothing has really changed about this person. No weight has been lost. Relationships with people who make the TV client crazy haven't all of a sudden disappeared. No extra money is coming into the household. Life work hasn't changed either. The only difference is that the person finally figured out how to *work with what is* and to *feel good about what is*, and that is truly a miracle. The reason for telling you about Stacy and Clinton's *What Not to Wear* program is because many of the guiding principles for dealing with life mistakes are the same as the guiding principles that Stacy and Clinton use for solving dressing mistakes.

- ♥ Stacy and Clinton teach acceptance of self and working with *what is* right now. You are learning to accept your own life energy, and you're developing a willingness to work with it right now.

- ♥ Stacy and Clinton stay focused on solving the fashion problem at hand. They put no energy into understanding or dealing with psychological/ emotional reasons why the problem exists. You are learning how to focus on the stopping solution and not get distracted or side-tracked with the mystery of *why* you have the problem.

♥ Stacy and Clinton throw out fashion mistakes because they can't be fixed and have no value. Today's lesson is the opportunity to reconsider the value of your life mistakes and to begin throwing them out because they have no value.

♥ Stacy and Clinton show how solving one important problem has a domino effect of improving many other aspects of life. You're learning that when you stop yourself, your life automatically works better, you like yourself better, and you open yourself to a spiritual awakening.

Without someone like Stacy or Clinton around to prod you, it's unlikely you'll toss your clothing mistakes. Unfortunately, it's unlikely you'll toss your life mistakes either. We love our mistakes and think they're very important and serious. The rehashing of past unpleasant experiences, past mistakes (either yours or someone else's) and past negative thinking is typically perceived as a mandatory step for personal healing and for the correction of mistakes. Right now your attachment to your own mistakes is a monumental obstacle standing in your way.

Considerable time and life energy is expended trying to interpret *why* things happened, *who's* at fault, *what* it means, and *what* to do about it all. If you 're seeing a therapist or feel inspired to go this route on your own, try to keep in mind that you are perceiving everything that happens to you through the filter of the ego. Ego always gives you a very good reason for hating yourself or another, and invariably you come to the unhappy conclusion the guilt or self-pity you feel for yourself or the anger you feel for another is justified. Disappointment in yourself or with someone in your world becomes a huge distraction, and it easily morphs into a reason for procrastinating and not stopping yourself. You did this bad thing or this bad thing happened in your life and now you're either tainted or wounded or sad and you can't stop until you get past it, and on and on. Your unhappy story gets bigger and more important and more fixed in your mind each time you retell it. Even worse, the unhappiness you feel from reliving your story creeps in to the present moment. So you have this fresh, beautiful moment to live and you let your unhappy story color it black. Here's the question to ask yourself: if your past was so unpleasant, why are you bringing it into the present moment? How exactly do you think your life will be better by doing this?

Mistakes and flaws are very interesting and mesmerizing. People find it fascinating to look at and talk about them. It's like reading a gotcha article in the *National Enquirer* or watching a sensational disaster on TV that gets played over and over and over again. With all this attention, you'd think mistakes have some inherent value, but they don't. A mistake is always a waste of energy, and waste has nothing to offer you. It's completely empty. Would you consider extracting a life lesson by hanging out in a pile of garbage? No, you wouldn't. A mistake is garbage, and you are not being smart when you expend your life energy standing in it. You are smart when you step out of the garbage.

A mistake has value only when it brings you to forgiveness, which is the topic of another lesson. Until then, consider the radical idea that a mistake is not the same as a solution. By putting all your attention on the mistake, you get more of the mistake. If you want the solution, that's where you have to focus your attention. It's always going to involve thinking something different and doing something different. So if you're looking at mistakes and analyzing them in an attempt to find a secret answer to your problem, you're looking in the wrong place. The answer isn't there.

It's possible, *but not common*, to make new and better stopping decisions for yourself without dwelling on your mistakes, without rehashing your unpleasant history, and without solving every other problem in your life that's a hold-over from the past. Think of how you drive a car. When you're sitting in the driver's seat, you're making driving decisions based on what's going on around you in the present moment. Is there a lot of traffic? Is it windy or rainy or snowy? Are you on a highway or a back road? Is the driver on your right texting or on the phone? Your driving decisions aren't based on what you did ten minutes ago, ten hours ago, ten days ago, or ten years ago. They're based on what's going on now. You might have other things in your life that aren't perfect, but you can still drive the car and respond appropriately to the present driving moment. Stopping yourself requires the exact same kind of present moment awareness. If your mind is stuck in the past, you can't help yourself because you aren't paying attention to what's going on now. You have to put your energy and attention on the present moment when the thought that you need something or when physical tension appears. That's where the work gets done.

A refusal to dwell on past mistakes or to be thrown off track by them isn't the same as repressing or ignoring them. It's making the conscious decision <u>not to give your energy</u> to something that has no useful function or purpose. If it gives you comfort or pleasure to dwell on the past, then swap out your sad story for a happy one. Recalling a happy moment in your past serves the purpose of making you happy now, and this is always helpful. Everyone has at least one happy memory to remember. Your exercise today is to extract it.

DAY 5 STOPPING PRACTICE

MIND: The skill of the mind is to make a decision and hold it.

1. Read your intention statement and write it in long-hand seven times. As always, make the act of concentrating on your words and writing them down an act of love. Try your best to make it as beautiful and legible as possible.

2. Say your intention out loud seven times.

3. Write a summary statement that reminds you what stopping looks like when it manifests in your life. Refer to your writing exercise for Day 3.

SPIRIT: The skill of the spirit is to experience an instant of inner peace so that you can turn off the ego and connect with your Christ-self.

Complete one 9-minute meditation period. Do it early in the morning, as soon as practical. When you're ready, sit in a comfortable private place, and allow yourself to relax. Then sit in stillness for another 60 seconds or longer if it feels comfortable to you.

Today's meditation phrase

The past is over. It can touch me not.

Write this prayer in your *Miracle Stopping Journal*:

I want to experience myself at peace.
I do not feel anxious or guilty because the Holy Spirit
will undo the consequences of any wrong decisions
that I made in the past if I let him.

HEART: The skill of the heart is to make self happy. Your happiness is the most important thing in the world and cannot be sacrificed for any reason.

Answer these questions:

1. Think about your happiest memories of the past. Briefly write about one.

2. Why did you pick this memory? What does it do for you?

BODY: The skill of the body is to use physical tension to diffuse physical tension.

Type exercise:	Aerobic
Activity:	<u>Brisk</u> walking
Time:	10 <u>consecutive</u> minutes, more is okay.

Write about your exercise experience: When, where, how-long, how you feel.

Day 6

LIES THAT HOLD YOU BACK

It's too hard

...nothing is difficult that is wholly desired.

A COURSE IN MIRACLES

Stopping is too hard.

Stopping is too complicated.

Stopping is an emotional downer.

Stopping takes the monumental strength of an Olympian.

Stopping is a multi-step process that requires special support or rehab services.

Stopping is only achievable for a few special, remarkable people.

Stopping is doubtful.

Some stopping problems are harder than others to solve.

You've heard these statements before, and they're all lies, popular, long-standing lies that you hear from high profile people, celebrity shrinks, authors of every kind, doctors, radio and TV show hosts and from the everyday people in your own life. You probably spout them too. You've heard and repeated the *it's so hard* lie about stopping for so long and so often, it doesn't occur to you to question it or to consider that it's just a collective opinion and not truth.

Lies are powerful because they block, fool or scare you. Consider the lie about the Earth being flat. Once upon a time, 500 years ago, most Earthlings thought the Earth was a horizontal plane, and that you could fall off the edge of it. Not everyone thought the world was flat, mind you, but most people thought it was. A large mass of believers fed the Earth-is-fat lie and kept it alive. Belief in the lie had an impact. The lie blocked exploration of the sea and the possibility of life on other continents. The lie increased fears about the risk of death and calamity when out in the ocean. And the lie made everyone think they understood the world and that they could accurately predict how things would turn out.

Your belief in the lie about hardness of stopping has an impact, too. It limits your idea about what you can accomplish. It increases your anxiety and fear about stopping. And it makes you think you know how poorly things are going to turn out. But you don't know how things are going to turn out. You aren't limited. And you aren't at risk of death or calamity.

Thinking about stopping is hard. Worrying about stopping is hard. Feeling bad about yourself while you procrastinate about stopping is hard. But the actual act of stopping yourself isn't as hard as you think it will be. Yes, it's different. Yes, you have to get used to the feeling of your own wild energy before it tames down. Yes, you have to be still instead of doing your unwanted behavior thing. So what if you're a little uncomfortable for a week or two while you diffuse your own tension. In the big scheme of things, it's a nit.

In our country stopping isn't recognized as a skill and is not taught, proactively, anywhere. This creates a lot of mystery and illusion around stopping. It leads to the perception that stopping is very special, very hard, very complicated and very important. In reality, stopping is completely ordinary and natural, and there's nothing special or important about it. It's highly unlikely you'll become famous or important when you learn how to stop yourself. Lots have people have done it. Maybe you'll get some attaboys from the people in your world; maybe you won't.

Chances are, right now, while you're reading this lesson, you're in stop mode. Chances are, right now, you're *not doing* the behavior you don't want to do. Is it a big deal? No. Does it require super human effort on your part? No. Is it natural and ordinary? Yes. You see, you already know how to stop yourself. You do. You know how to stop yourself for a least a second. And if know how to stop yourself for a second, you can stop yourself for two seconds. And if you can stop yourself for two seconds, you can stop yourself for three seconds. And if you can stop yourself for three seconds, you can stop yourself for a minute. If you can stop yourself a minute, you can stop yourself an hour. An hour turns into a day, and a day turns into a week, and a week turns into a month, and a month turns into a year. All that's ever required is that you stop yourself for a second, followed by another second and another and another.

Stopping is just another simple self-maintenance task that you perform for yourself. You brush your teeth. You shampoo your hair. You change your clothes. You take out the trash. All of these tasks require diligence and effort, but none of them are too hard for you. No monumental, killer stopping effort is ever asked of you either.

Do yourself a favor, and quit telling yourself stopping is hard.

DAY 6 STOPPING PRACTICE

MIND: The skill of the mind is to make a decision and hold it.

1. Read your intention statement and write it out in long-hand ten times. As always, make concentrating on your writing an act of love and purpose.

2. Say your intention out loud ten times, slowly.

3. Answer these questions about your experience with stopping:

    - During the course of your entire life, estimate how many seconds you've stopped yourself?

    - What made it possible for you to stop yourself for these seconds?

    - What do you already know about stopping?

    - What can you say to yourself instead of stopping is hard?

SPIRIT: The skill of the spirit is to experience an instant of inner peace so that you can turn off the ego and connect with your Christ-self.

Sit in a comfortable, private place and slowly repeat today's phrase for a full 10-minute period. Then sit in stillness for another 60 seconds or longer if it feels comfortable to you.

Today's meditation phrase

Let me not see myself as limited.

Write this prayer in your *Miracle Stopping Journal.*

I am not weak, but strong.
I am not helpless, but all powerful.
I am not limited, but unlimited.
I am not doubtful, but certain.
I am not an illusion, but a reality.
I cannot see in darkness, but in light.

HEART: The skill of the heart is to make self happy. Your happiness is the most important thing in the world and cannot be sacrificed for any reason.

Pretend you're already highly successful at stopping yourself and someone who's struggling with stopping asked you for advice about how to do it. What advice would you give this person about the best, most efficient way to stop yourself? Why does it make you happy to give this advice?

BODY: The skill of the body is to use physical tension to diffuse physical tension.

If needed, go to www.powertostop.com/tools for instruction.

Type Exercise: Flexibility

Activity: Stretching of all major joints

Time: 6-10 minutes

Write about your exercise experience: When, where, how-long, how you feel.

Day 7

REVIEW OF WEEK ONE

*If different abilities are applied long enough to one goal,
the abilities themselves become unified. This is because
they are channelized in one direction, or in one way.*

A COURSE IN MIRACLES

Review days occur every seventh day in the stopping program. Reviews help you to remember your accomplishments during the previous week, and they help you to reinforce and consolidate key ideas. New ideas are not introduced on review days.

Week one accomplishments

♥ You learned the four stopping skills and practiced them every day.

♥ You asked for a healing miracle.

♥ You created a stopping intention.

♥ You developed basic awareness of harmlessness and energy conservation.

♥ You looked at your tendency to go to the dark side to get what you want.

♥ You reconsidered the concept of hardness.

DAY 7 STOPPING PRACTICE

MIND: The skill of the mind is to make a decision and hold it.

1. Write out your stopping intention 10 times.

2. Say your stopping intention out loud 10 times.

3. Review the ideas you examined for mind training this week. Which idea was the most meaningful or helpful to you? Explain why.

SPIRIT: The skill of the spirit is to experience an instant of inner peace so that you can turn off the ego and connect with your Christ self.

Read the six meditation phrases that were provided during the week. Pick the one that's most meaningful for you, follow the time directions associated with the phrase, and use it for your meditation today.

Write this phrase in your *Miracle Stopping Journal* and explain why it's important to you.

HEART: The skill of the heart is to make self happy. Your happiness is the most important thing in the world and cannot be sacrificed for any reason.

This week you rediscovered many simple, effective ways to make yourself happy. In fact, you did something every single day to experience at least a moment of happiness. Think about the amount of time and effort you expended making yourself happy each day, and then estimate your total weekly time investment in your own happiness. There's a relationship between effort and happiness. Write about your impression of this relationship in your *Miracle Stopping Journal*. Which happiness activity was most enjoyable and worked best for you?

BODY: The skill of the body is to use physical tension to diffuse physical tension.

Physical rest day. No activity required.

Write about your weekly experience with physical activity.

- ♥ Did you begin to discipline yourself to be active?
- ♥ Which type of activity did you like the best?
- ♥ What kind of relaxation result did you get, if any?

RATE YOUR WEEK:

Use a scale of (1) low to (10) high. Rate your weekly experience on the program, and briefly explain why you gave this rating.

What are you doing well?

What can you do better?

Day 8

SET ONE BOUNDARY

A boundary is not a sacrifice

There is no need to learn through pain. And gentle
lessons are acquired joyously and remembered gladly.

A COURSE IN MIRACLES

Stopping begins by setting one boundary for yourself, a firm one. Here it is. No indulging yourself with excess food. No drinking. No drugging. No smoking. No mindless hook-up sexing. No doing whatever it is you don't want to do. Not even a little. You say no to yourself whether or not you feel like saying no. You say no to yourself if you're having a bumpy time in your primary relationships right now. You say no to yourself if your job is stressful. You say no to yourself if a hurricane with the force of Katrina makes a flood in your house. You say no to yourself if the stock market crashes or if you win the lottery. You say no to yourself if you're tense and uncomfortable and you're having the worst day of your life. No is your boundary. There is no condition, and there is no reason where this boundary is inappropriate. You are not exempt from saying no to yourself, no matter what.

Your exit from hell is based on drawing this one firm line for yourself. It's easier to make an uncompromising and unwaivering *no* decision than it is to make a decision based on containment, where *a little* of the substance is sometimes okay. For one thing, it's easier to minimize or eliminate your impulsive tendency when the substance isn't in your body. Once the substance enters your bloodstream, your own physiology starts working against you with stronger and more urgent cravings. Your choice to use *a little* is the choice to put craziness in your body. You can't be *a little* crazy. You're either crazy or not. Crazy, impulsive behavior is what you're trying to minimize, and it makes no sense to aggravate your own problem or make it worse. Then there's the fact that using *a little* of the substance clouds your mind and makes it exceedingly easy to forget about just having *a little*. Before you know it, WTF mentality takes over and you don't really care what you do. Unfortunately, a WTF mentality brings about a WTF result, and it's always the result you don't want. *Just say no.* It's the sanest, swiftest, most efficient way to break free.

Saying no is also accomplished by avoiding social situations that pressure you to cross your own boundary. When you expose yourself to self-destructive activities, you're taking a risk and putting yourself in danger. It's smarter and more practical to pre-empt danger and stay out of the sphere of influence of others, especially when you're just starting out on the stopping path. There will come a time when your stopping intention is so strong, it doesn't matter where you are or who you're with, but this is not that time.

Pre-empting danger might mean not going to a bar after work. Or not going to an all-you-can-eat restaurant. Or not hanging out with your buddies for a while. Or not accepting a date that will end in unwanted sex. Learning how to say no to others is exactly the same as saying no to yourself. You're not a leaf in the wind, blowing this way or that with no direction. You have a direction because you know what you want. You want to stop. Your stopping goal strategically guides you to make yourself unavailable to the whims and desires of others. Engaging in something just because you can or just because it's there is a meaningless waste of life. When asked why he dallied with Monica Lewinsky, former president Bill Clinton said, *because I could.* I ask you, dear reader, how did that work out for him?

Occasionally your stopping intention might disappoint or bother others who are used to your former expression of indulgence. You don't have to explain yourself or ask others for their support. You don't have to get angry at people for tempting you, either. Your job is not to judge or correct your brothers and sisters. Your job is to say no. A simple no is all it takes. It's quick. It's easy, and it doesn't have to involve drama, emotional turmoil or anger. Today's stopping practice provides the opportunity to creatively think about how you can say no to others. Your task is to get comfortable communicating *no* to others in a way that's spontaneous and natural for you.

The word *stopping* is a better word choice than *abstaining* or *quitting*. Stopping is a life skill you give yourself. Abstaining and quitting are about giving something up, which is a sacrifice. Sacrifice is one of the oldest human concepts and is closely associated with religion. There are remnants of sacrificial altars to God in ancient sites all over the world, and there are remnants of sacrificial religious practices still in use today, such as fasting or giving something up for lent at Easter time. Muslim extremists who carry out suicide attacks, operate under the principle that suffering is important to God and is rewarded by Him.

We all know the deal with sacrifice. It's a dirty little bargain you make with God. If you suffer and give up something of value for God, He'll do something nice for you. He'll grant you a wish or bring rain for the crops or He'll forgive your badness and grant you eternal salvation in heaven. The bigger the value of the thing you give up, the bigger the reward from God. On the surface the practice of bargaining with God seems harmless, but it isn't because it engenders fear, and it makes God very scary. What horrible bad thing is God going to ask of you? Why would a loving God want you to suffer or die? How could a loving God put a condition on your worthiness? When you're in the dark business of making a sacrificial bargain with God, you're worried that He's mean, vengeful and judgmental, and you think you need a way to get in His good graces to appease Him. It's the unacknowledged belief that you're not lovable as you are, *right now*, and that you have to do something to make up for it. This unwholesome, unworthy message secretly guides you through your life, and it all starts right here, with your fundamental ideas about God.

Our God stories have been around for thousands of years. We've heard them so often and from so many respected sources, the fearful messages are accepted without examination or question. We think we're *supposed* to be afraid of God, and that fear is a sign of devotion and fidelity, but is it? Do you like to hang out with people and things that scare you? No, you run and hide from them and join in where you feel more accepted. It's not possible to undo a lifetime of conditioning in a few paragraphs, but it is possible to at least consider a new, fearless and wholly loving interpretation of God. From the first page of this book I've been introducing you to the concept that love is harmless. If God is love and love is harmless, then God must be harmless. Sacrifice cannot be *of* God because sacrifice is the idea of loss and harm. Sacrifice must therefore come from ego and not from God.

Stopping is <u>not</u> sacrifice. It's gain. You gain by restoring your mind to a clear and unimpeded channel for the Christ that resides within. It's enough of a challenge to give your time and your awareness to the Christ-self under normal life circumstances. Your to-do list, your relationships and daily world drama all compete for your attention. It takes willingness and resolve to cut through all this and make the connection. A sedated and dull mind enables you to forget your willingness, and it blocks communication. You cannot hear the Voice for God when your mind is off-line. The connecting device has to be up and running. Being in control of your mind also restores your sanity. The experience of self as a crazy, out-of-control person who does and says crazy, out-of-control things is immediately undone. Craziness is a scary, unpredictable way of being that makes you afraid of yourself. It makes others afraid of you, too. The return to right-mindedness is not a little thing.

The only sacrifice you're asked to make is the fearful, false idea that you need excess food or a substance to be relaxed and happy. God did not create your needy thought, and so it cannot be real. We treat our thoughts like they're all-important pearls of wisdom that are worth keeping, but they're not. Some ideas should be thrown out or changed, and your false needy idea is of them. When you were a child you thought you needed your Teddy Bear to feel happy and safe. When you grew up, you realized you didn't need it at all. You don't need your unwanted behavior to make you feel safe either.

DAY 8 STOPPING PRACTICE

MIND: The skill of the mind is to make a decision and hold it.

1. Write out your stopping intention one time and study it for a moment. Do you need to make any changes to keep it fresh or to make it more exciting? If you do, make the change and then write your intention again. Put your full concentration into the act of writing your intention.

2. Say your stopping intention out loud three times in front of a mirror.

3. This week you'll create and use a simple visualization tool where you see yourself actively *rejecting* the excess food, substance or behavior that you indulge in. Your goal today is to create the visualization. There are three scenes, and each one only takes a few seconds. Altogether, the visualization won't take more than 15 seconds to play in your mind. Visualization is a proven technique used by world class athletes and other high performers. It's about making a new pattern in your mind and following the pattern.

Scene #1: Envision yourself in the most typical situation where you indulge your unwanted behavior. The scene should either be the *point of purchase* or the moment *just before* you indulge.

Scene #2: Now see yourself doing something physically active that *rejects* or *pushes away* the indulgence. It could be driving by. Walking away. Dumping something in the garbage. Throwing something in the sink. Flushing it down the toilet. Putting your hands over your mouth. This scene will be personal to you and to your situation. Pick whatever image works for you.

Scene #3: See yourself smiling after you perform the rejection scene.

Put the three scenes together and play them in your mind a few times until the complete, 3-scene visualization can be done in 15 seconds or less.

SPIRIT: The skill of the spirit is to experience an instant of inner peace so that you can turn off the ego and connect with your Christ self.

Today's practice is one 7-minute meditation period, one 3-minute meditation period, plus at least 10 recitations of the meditation phrase throughout the day. Do your first meditation early in the morning, as soon as practical. Do the second one whenever it works for your schedule. Keep track of your recitations in your *Miracle Stopping Journal.*

Today's meditation phrase

I can give up but what was never real.

HEART: The skill of the heart is to make self happy. Your happiness is the most important thing in the world and cannot be sacrificed for any reason.

You make yourself happy by setting a simple stopping boundary for yourself and by saying no to people and situations that put you at risk to self-destruct. Saying no to others may or may not involve words, an explanation or a direct approach. In every case, saying no is expressed in a calm and unemotional way, without blaming, apologizing or creating drama.

Think of three or more ways to say no. Write them down now so you'll have a response prepared in your mind before you need it.

BODY: The skill of the body is to use physical tension to diffuse physical tension.

Here's an overview of your activity schedule for week two:

Day 8	*Day 9*	*Day 10*	*Day 11*	*Day 12*	*Day 13*	*Day 14*
Aerobic	*Strength*	*Aerobic*	*Strength*	*Aerobic*	*Flexibility*	*Off*

Type exercise: Aerobics

Activity: <u>Brisk</u> walking

Time: 15 <u>continuous</u> minutes

If you have a pedometer, put it on in the morning and wear it all day. At the end of the day, write down the number of steps you took. This is you're starting point.

Write about your exercise experience. Explain when you did it, where you did it, and how it felt.

Day 9

HAPPINESS BEYOND YOUR WILDEST EXPECTATIONS

Find your passion

In you is all of Heaven. Every leaf that falls is given life in you.
Each bird that ever sang will sing again in you. And every flower
that ever bloomed has saved its perfume and its loveliness for you.
A COURSE IN MIRACLES

I publish and host the StoppingNation blog, and because of this I'm always on the prowl for high quality content about substance abuse, compulsions and unwanted behaviors. One thing I've noticed is that people constantly make platitudes about how stopping takes courage, but no one ever explains exactly *why* courage is required. To be truthful, the actual act of stopping is ordinary and not courageous at all. The thing that requires courage is the prospect of coming face to face with your own unhappiness after you stop yourself. These feelings, so long denied, will always surface.

Bravery is acting in a fearless way even though you're really afraid. In this case, bravery is demonstrated by your willingness to accept and experience your own unhappy feelings. The hardest part is to have your unhappy feelings without being blown away by them. Lessen your fear by recognizing that some transitional unhappiness comes with the territory. You can feel unhappy without creating drama around it or without going into a big panic. Of course, you can always skip this step and take an anti-anxiety drug or a happy pill. But that doesn't solve the problem, does it? What difference does it make if the substance you're using to alter your mind is a medical prescription or a form of self-medication? All you get from your prescription is an easy, socially-acceptable way to dull your pain, procrastinate and not deal with your unhappiness a while longer. Oh, and you get to fool yourself, too, because you're still vigilantly holding on to the magical belief that you need to put something in your body to be happy.

Your unhappiness can serve the purpose of leading you to your happiness. Deep inside your unhappiness is a nugget of gold. Misery leads to your un-misery. Problems lead to solutions. The decision to get happy comes from being unhappy. That's the way it works. When you allow yourself to feel your own unhappiness, a moment miraculously arises when you conclude there must be a better way to go through life. It's a hallelujah moment, and it's also the turning point when you finally get inspired to *do something* about making yourself happy. If you continue to avoid your own unhappy feelings, you miss out on the powerful propulsion that takes you out of it. Give yourself the satisfaction of changing from a sad state of mind to a happy one under your own horse power. You are not your unhappy feelings, and this is what you will come to discover if you give yourself half a chance. Trust that you *will* figure it out.

A large part of getting yourself happy is learning how to deal with disappointment. There will always be disappointment to transcend. It comes with being an Earthling. Parents disappoint. Spouses disappoint. Children disappoint. Friends disappoint. Employers disappoint. Politicians disappoint. Doctors disappoint. Religious leaders disappoint. Weather disappoints. Pick any human experience, and it can disappoint you. If, like most people, you expect the world and the people in it to make you happy, there will be no way to mitigate your disappointments. Your unhappiness will be legendary. Our world is ego-land, and well, an ego is an ego. It will only make you happy for a price. Even if you faithfully do *your part* and play the role assigned to you by other egos, you will still be unsatisfied and disappointed because you're playing a role instead of living a meaningful life.

This is why it's essential to find a more creative way to deal with disappointment, or you will forever be stuck in self-pity. The ticket to happiness is to discover and develop the thing you like to do that makes your heart sing regardless of what's being provided or withheld by others. This activity is your passion and purpose. In addition to making your own life a more joyful experience, your passion and purpose is a powerful shield for deflecting disappointment. A shield blocks destructive forces from hitting you. Or said another way, a shield is a barrier that stands in between you and something that has the potential to make you unhappy. This lessens the impact of the negative force. Typically, a shield is something like a helmet or a bullet-proof vest or a tank, but a strong, meaningful life purpose is also a shield because it keeps you going when unhappy situations crop up. And they *will* crop up.

In *Baby Grand*, singer/songwriter Billy Joel writes about how music is his personal shield for deflecting disappointments. Joel's song tells us how friends come and go. Fame comes and goes, money comes and goes, women come and go; but Joel's own passion for music never changes. This passion, which is symbolized by his baby grand piano, is a reliable and constant source of happiness for Joel. The bottom line is that you have to find your own baby grand piano, your own passionate purpose in life. Disappointments can't be avoided, but a strong passion and purpose gives you something else to focus on. It takes your attention off what isn't working, and puts it on what is. This is how to make yourself happy when everything else in your life stalls out.

Your life is not a random, meaningless experience, but you may be living in a way that's meaningless, where your purpose for being here is not clear to you. Hopelessness and despair come from shuffling through life without knowing why. Of course, this makes you unhappy! Who wouldn't be unhappy? If you're experiencing persistent unhappiness, chances are you've either forgotten your purpose or you haven't taken time to discover it. There's no specific formula for finding your purpose in life, but it often relates to things you're naturally good at, things you enjoy doing, and something you feel strongly about. Today's stopping practice provides the opportunity to think about your purpose and to at least figure out what you want to do more of.

Clarity about your life purpose ignites your energy. It takes a ho-hum life experience and kicks it up several notches. When was the last time you couldn't wait to get up in the morning? This kind of *bring it on* feeling of aliveness comes to you, automatically, when you live on purpose and with purpose, and it's the first sign that you're on the right track. Losing sense of time is another important sign. When you're fully engaged in doing whatever it is you love doing, time doesn't matter. The momentary suspension of time is like a tiny brush with eternity because it's like being in heaven where there is no time.

Your true nature is happiness because your true nature is your Christ-self, which has no darkness. Happiness is there inside you now, but it's underneath the garbage you have not deflected and it's trapped in the meaningful life you have not expressed. Dig it out, and do it as an act of self-love. When you experience your own happiness and when you extend it to the world, you are Love in action. People will be magnetized by your happiness and love. Things will come to you more easily. Problems will resolve themselves more easily. Try it and see for yourself if this is true.

May today be the day that you're happy and you know it. Clap. Clap. Clap.

DAY 9 STOPPING PRACTICE

MIND: The skill of the mind is to make a decision and hold it.

1. Slowly write out your stopping intention three times.

2. Slowly say your intention out loud three times in front of a mirror.

3. Review the three-scene rejection visualization that you created yesterday. Make whatever refinements or improvements that are needed. Remember you should be able to play the entire visualization in 15 seconds or less.

4. Play your visualization in your mind three times. Altogether, this will take less than 2 minutes.

SPIRIT: The skill of the spirit is to experience an instant of inner peace so that you can turn off the ego and connect with your Christ self.

Today's practice is one 8-minute meditation period, one 2-minute meditation period and 10 recitations of the meditation phrase throughout the day. Do your first meditation early in the morning, as soon as practical. Do the second one whenever it works for your schedule. Keep track of your recitations in your *Miracle Stopping Journal*.

Today's meditation phrase

God's Will for me is perfect happiness.

HEART: The skill of the heart is to make self happy. Your happiness is the most important thing in the world and cannot be sacrificed for any reason.

You came here, to planet Earth, to do something. What is it? When will you allow yourself to do it? The questions that follow will get you to think about activities that are meaningful to you so that you can begin to do more of them. This will make you happy. Before you begin the exercise, be sure to get in a quiet, relaxed meditative state of mind so that your Christ-self is accessed and your Truth easily flows through.

1. What things am I naturally good at?

2. What things do I most enjoy doing, regardless of whether money or glory is involved?

3. What kind of companionship do I most enjoy? (*Individuals, groups, animals, solitude*)

4. What do I feel strongly about, if anything?

5. What qualities and characteristics do I most value in myself and others?

Flip back and check your *skill of the heart* answers to Day 2 and Day 5 for additional clues about yourself and write them down for handy reference.

BODY: The skill of the body is to use physical tension to diffuse physical tension.

If needed, go to www.powertostop.com/tools for instruction.

Type exercise:	Strength Training
Activity:	Warm-up
	Core conditioning
	Upper body conditioning
Time:	15 minutes

Pedometer people: Increase your daily steps by 250. At the end of the day, record your actual step performance in your *Miracle Stopping Journal.*

Write about your exercise experience. Explain when you did it, where you did it, and how it felt.

Day 10

THE SPIRITUAL WARRIOR'S CALL

Awaken from the dream of life

You are not yet awake, but you can learn how to awaken.

A COURSE IN MIRACLES

A warrior is someone who fights battles as a way of life. All warriors have the same goal: to conquer and defeat the enemy. To win! Battles change from one era to another, from one country to another, but the goal of winning never changes. The difference between a worldly warrior and a spiritual warrior has to do with the type of battle that's fought. Worldly warriors fight battles with other worldly warriors. They fight to win tangible things like land, money, power and glory. Whereas spiritual warriors are concerned with just one thing: winning over the ever-present urge to self-destruct that comes from the ego. It's the only worthy battle, and spiritual warriors are determined to win it.

Our worldly life on Earth is the ego's domain. From the moment our life begins, we begin to experience the ego's downward pull of gravity, which is negativity and death. Earthly experiences always involve either the witnessing or the direct experience of injustice, treachery, catastrophe, and human misery of every kind. These dramatic scenarios are intended to invoke feelings of helplessness, injustice and emotional turbulence. Ego gets stronger and feeds on the tension and emotional churning resulting from these disturbing events. The spiritual warrior seeks freedom from slavery to the ego, which is partially achieved through freedom from tension and bad feelings. He knows that anxiety, angst and drama do not solve problems or uplift self or the world out of a negative place and into a positive one. His or her strategic mission is to conserve energy and to stay alive by eliminating or at least minimizing predatory and volatile states of mind. Ego generates constant tension and discord by juxtaposing the way life is supposed to be with the way life is. The way life is supposed to be is a dream, a fantasy, and we're all having it. The dream goes something like this:

Once upon a time, not so long ago, a special child was born. By the strangest coincidence, the child has your name, your characteristics, and your history, and he/she grew up to be you. The grown-up you is adored by everyone, and you routinely get treated as a special and privileged being. In fact, the people in your world all have the same life purpose: they exist to make you happy. Experiences like discomfort, loneliness, anxiety or frustration are totally unknown to you because your needs are forecasted and attended to by others. You don't have to bother with loving yourself because someone else does this for you. You're constantly entertained and pleased, and you never have to do a thing for yourself, including the mildest work of changing a crappy thought to a happy one.

Somehow you know you're dreaming this scenario, but it's such a lovely dream you don't want it to stop, and you know you can keep it going as long as you want. All you have to do is stay asleep. Then wham! An intruder screams in your ear, whacks you on the head, and jumps wildly on your bed. You whine and put up a mighty protest, but the disruption continues. Your dream story has three possible endings. Ending #1: You feel sorry for yourself and get justifiably angry at the intruder for screwing up your dream. You spend the rest of your life in misery trying to figure out why your dream didn't work out and who's at fault. Ending #2: You realize you have the power to create a different and better dream. You spend the rest of your life making your new dream come true with a more willing cast of characters who aren't so disruptive. Ending #3: You stop dreaming and wake up.

A fairy tale is a fairy tale. Some fairy tales are nightmares and some have happy endings. Sure you can dream a better dream, but a dream is still an illusion, not the truth. It takes considerable energy to maintain the illusion that the fantasy of special love is true. Consider the way you expend your own life energy. You're either pining for the dream of special love, protecting your dream of special love, analyzing all the defects in your special love relationships, feeling guilty or mad about how your special dreams didn't work out, reliving past special dreams, conjuring up new ones, coercing people to conform to your dream requirements. This list goes on and on. The preoccupation with dreaming never ends.

There's an old Neil Sedaka song from the 60's about breaking up being hard to do. Well, waking up is hard to do, too. The problem is that we can't wake ourselves. Someone else is needed to nudge us out of Snoozeland. Enter the people who disillusion and disappoint. These are the people with the biggest dream-busting potential. The average person gets very sad, mad or put out with dream-busters because the average person doesn't want to wake up. That's why we're still here on Earth instead of in Heaven with God where there are no dreams. The Spiritual Warrior has a profound advantage over the average person because he/she has answered the Call to awaken. Each pin-prick of disappointment deflates the dream of life. Instead of resisting *what is*, and thereby generating conflict and tension, life experience is accepted without masking it or correcting it. Dis-illusion literally means no illusion or no dream. A spiritual warrior defies gravity and maintains inner peace by perceiving disappointments and disillusions from a higher perspective, as a tool for transformation. As luck would have it, there's an abundance of disappointment and disillusion to be had. This assures an effortless and comprehensive training program. There's no need to drop everything and become a monk or to live in isolation.

The spiritual warrior uses disappointments to wake up. You are a spiritual warrior.

DAY 10 STOPPING PRACTICE

MIND: The skill of the mind is to make a decision and hold it.

1. Slowly write out your stopping intention four times.

2. Slowly say your intention out loud four times in front of a mirror.

3. Play your rejection visualization in your mind four times.

4. Answer this question:

What is the Call to awaken and when will you answer it?

SPIRIT: The skill of the spirit is to experience an instant of inner peace so that you can turn off the ego and connect with your Christ self.

Today's practice is one 9-minute meditation period, one 1 minute meditation period, plus 10 recitations of the meditation phrase throughout the day. Do your long meditation early in the morning, as soon as practical. Do the other one whenever you can fit it in. Keep track of your recitations in your *Miracle Stopping Journal.*

Today's meditation phrase

All things are lessons God would have me learn.

HEART: The skill of the heart is to make self happy. Your happiness is the most important thing in the world and cannot be sacrificed for any reason.

Use your answers from yesterday to make a first pass at defining your passion and purpose in life. A fill-in-the-blanks model is provided below, but you are welcome to substitute any other process or statement that feels right to you.

I use my natural talents of _____ and _____ (*things you're already good at*) to engage _____ (*individuals, groups, or animals*) in _____ and _____ (*things you most enjoy doing*) to

_____ *(the thing you feel strongly about)* so that the experiences of _____ *(the life qualities you most value)* come to me.

Consolidate your answers into a sentence. Without thinking about it too much, make whatever changes come to you as you're writing your sentence out.

BODY: The skill of the body is to use physical tension to diffuse physical tension.

Type exercise:	Aerobics
Activity:	<u>Brisk</u> walking
Time:	15 <u>continuous</u> minutes

Pedometer people: Add another 250 steps today. This is plus

500 steps from your starting point. At the end of the day, record your actual step performance in your *Miracle Stopping Journal.*

Write about your exercise experience. Explain when you did it, where you did it, and how it felt.

ANOTHER LIE THAT HOLDS YOU BACK

You're sick

Health is the result of relinquishing all attempts to use the body lovelessly.
A COURSE IN MIRACLES

A lot of out-of-control behaviors are commonly labeled as disease, especially when the behavior is extreme. That said, the question about whether substance abuse and/or out-of-control behaviors are a disease or a life process problem is still a hotly debated item, and the answer you get depends on who you're talking to. A recently published special health report on *Overcoming Addictions* produced by The Harvard Medical School doesn't make a definitive claim one way or another. Their bland conclusion is that that everyone with an addiction suffers and that addictions have a biological component. That said, the disease model is by far the most prevalent and popular opinion.

Our culture makes it exceedingly easy to buy into the disease model. Americans expect to get sick; they expect physicians to be involved in the recovery process; and they expect to take medicines to restore health and wellness. Every single day the TV bombards us with sicko messages from big pharma companies. From the time we wake up until the time we go to sleep, we hear how unhealthy we are. It's relentless. If you really listen to the symptoms of disease that get rattled off, you'll quickly discover that it's almost impossible not to have one. We even know the acronyms for common diseases. ED means erectile dysfunction. COPD means chronic obstructive pulmonary disease. RA means rheumatoid arthritis, and on and on. And all those side effects? Oh my goodness, it's enough to make you stay well.

The claimed solution for every health problem is a drug of some kind. Depressed, take a drug. Too fat, take a drug. Can't sleep, take a drug. Got the heebie jeebies, take a drug. The drug promises to make you feel better, and it promises to give you a happier, more affectionate life experience. Just look at the images of the people taking drugs. After they take the prescription drug, they're always smiling and happy and hugging each other. No matter what the underlying health problem happens to be, the take home message is always the same: You're a sick person. Go to your doctor. Tell him to give you this drug. You need a drug for your health. You need a drug for your happiness.

The lure of sickness is compounded and reinforced by experts and pundits who appear on TV talk shows. The commentator's job is to judge the behavior of celebrities and ordinary people, label it as sick, and prescribe *getting help*, medical treatments or other interventions. Commentators are always good looking, well-dressed people. They always have relevant credentials and a high-profile life. Who dares to dispute an expert when he/she says that a celebrity behaving badly is sick? But here's the question you have to ask yourself. When you hear that a celebrity gone wild is *sick* are you thinking good things about this person or not-so-good things about this person? Saying that someone is *sick* for out-of-control behaviors is the new, politically correct way of saying the person is bad, weak, or making a mess of life.

For sure, embracing the concept of disease has helped millions of people in 12-step programs, and who can argue with that kind of success? For sure, you need to be *officially* designated as sick to take advantage of insurance coverage and reimbursement. That's a no brainer. But something else is going on here. There's something hiding behind the disease debate, and it's a secret affinity for being sick. I remember once when I was a little girl I was sick with either measles or chicken pox, one of those childhood diseases that's rarely seen anymore. My Mom doted on me and pampered me and let me sleep in her bed the whole time I was sick. Even though I was hot and sweaty and uncomfortable, I loved it. In fact, it's one of my fondest memories of her.

There's something strangely comforting and blameless about having a disease, isn't there? The disease label gives you a stake in the ground to hang on to for safety. *Now I know what my problem is, I'm sick.* And it removes you from taking responsibility for what's happening in your life. *Poor you, you're sick. Such a pity you got stuck with it.* Disease is one of those random things that you can't help. The problem is that you were born with your addictive genes and you had your chaotic childhood and now you're in an emotionally charged and toxic environment that makes those out-of-control behaviors blossom into a full-fledged disease. You have the world's biggest and best excuse for everything. You could have a great life and be a great person except *this damned disease got you.* Being sick gives you a special status in the world, invites special attention, and exempts you from performing. Oh yeah, that's definitely worth being sick.

There's no question that food and/or substance abuse has the potential to modify the way your brain operates, which then decreases functionality and exacerbates the problem. This isn't the issue. The biggest problem with the disease model is that it confuses cause and effect. All self-attack and all self-wasting behaviors make you sick. Or said another way, anything you consistently do to harm yourself is the *cause* that's going to *result* in disease. The body, after all, is not indestructible. If you stay out in the sun for 12 hours a day for 12 years, you're likely to get skin cancer. If you consistently have unprotected sex with multiple partners, you're likely to get an STD. If you eat like a pig every day of your life, you're likely to get obese and develop heart disease and/or diabetes. If you smoke like a chimney, you're likely to get lung cancer. If you engage in a behavior that alters your state of mind, you're likely to develop a brain disease or disorder that reflects this behavior.

It seems so obvious, doesn't it? Sickness is the natural, ordinary by-product of repetitive wasting behaviors, and healing is the natural, ordinary by-product of stopping the wasting behavior. Here are some common everyday examples that show how wasting is the potent seed that ultimately manifests in disease.

♥ Brushing your teeth is a normal self-care of activity. If you don't brush your teeth every day, your gums recede and gum disease presents itself. Gum disease and tooth decay is a direct result of not loving yourself enough to take care of yourself. *Conclusion:* gum disease is not the cause of self-neglect. Self-neglect is the cause of gum disease.

♥ Shampooing your hair is a normal self-care activity. If you don't shampoo your hair on a regular basis, your hair gets greasy, you scalp gets scaly, and you create an environment that invites bacteria and parasites. Hair loss and scalp disease result from lack of attention and care to hair. *Conclusion:* scalp disease is not the cause of self-neglect. Self-neglect is the cause of scalp disease.

♥ Taking out the trash every day or so is a normal self-care activity. If you don't take out the trash, it quickly piles up. Your house stinks. Rodents and insects come to live there, and it's highly likely that many diseases linked to lack of sanitation present themselves. *Conclusion:* Lack of sanitation results in disease. Disease does not result in lack of sanitation.

Despite the obvious connection between wasting behaviors and disease, many people prefer to embrace the disease model, the idea that your sickness is causing your behavior. You may be one of them. For the time being, do an experiment and put your disease preference aside. As much as practical and possible, try to minimize the amount of your energy you give to the concept of being sick. Don't indulge it. Don't use it to get something from others. Don't talk about it. Refrain from using the labels of disease like *addict* or *in recovery*. The more you repeat these labels, the more you believe in them.

The best way to develop faith in your own healing is to act like you're normal, *as if* you don't have a disease. Devoted parents with sick and handicapped kids go out of their way to make sure school systems mainstream their kids and treat them normally, *as if* the disease/handicap didn't exist. The disease/handicap can easily result in a contracted, lesser life experience and a lower expectation of performance, and many parents vigorously resist these limits for their kids. They want their kid to have the same A-list experience that normal kids are having, not the D-list experience. Perhaps there's a clue here about how to proceed.

> You can be your own devoted parent
> You can ignore your so-called disease
> You can proceed *as if* you're normal.

> Will you?

DAY 11 STOPPING PRACTICE

MIND: The skill of the mind is to make a decision and hold it.

1. Slowly write out your stopping intention six times.

2. Slowly say your intention out loud six times in front of a mirror.

3. Play your rejection visualization in your mind three times.

4. *Answer these two questions:*

Be honest with yourself. What do you like about accepting the label of disease?

How does refusing the disease label help you to minimize or undo your impulse to self-destruct, if at all?

SPIRIT: The skill of the spirit is to experience an instant of inner peace so that you can turn off the ego and connect with your Christ self.

Today's practice is two 6-minute meditation periods. Do your first meditation early in the morning, as soon as practical. Do the other one whenever it's convenient and fits into your schedule. Use the meditation phrase throughout the day, whenever you need it.

Today's meditation phrase

My holiness shines bright and clear today.

HEART: The skill of the heart is to make self happy. Your happiness is the most important thing in the world and cannot be sacrificed for any reason.

Imagine you can have anything you want to make yourself happy. Anything at all. The sky is the limit. The one and only thing you have to do to get it is figure out what's wanted. This is your chance to be a kid again and indulge your heart's desire. Kids ask for what they want without worrying if it's possible or reasonable or affordable or anything else. Give yourself permission to be petty or grand. Put down every detail. This includes every desire you secretly hope to have fulfilled, every scrap of special attention or affection you would like to experience. Don't leave anything out, whether it's worldly or spiritual. There's no right or wrong answer. There's only your unexpressed, secret longing that wants to come out and be noticed.

Give yourself permission to have what you want.

BODY: The skill of the body is to use physical tension to diffuse physical tension.

Go to *www.powertostop.com/tools* for instruction, if needed.

Type exercise:	Strength Training
Activity:	Warm-up
	Core conditioning
	Lower body conditioning
Time:	15 minutes (or longer)

Pedometer people: Add 250 steps today. This is +750 steps from your starting point. At the end of the day, record the total number of steps you took in your *Miracle Stopping Journal.*

As usual, make a comment about your activity experience.

Day 12

THE POWER SKILL OF THE SPIRIT

Peace diffuses tension

There is a place in you where there is perfect peace.
There is a place where nothing is impossible. There
is a place in you where the strength of God abides.

A COURSE IN MIRACLES

The practice of inner peace is one of the four fundamental power skills for stopping yourself. From Day 1 of the *Power to Stop* program, you've been conditioning yourself to develop a value for inner peace and to sit still and *do nothing* except calm your mind with fearless, loving thoughts. A peaceful state of mind leads to a more peaceful and less agitated physical experience. Obviously, this is an important stopping strategy. Even more, a moment of peace is the actual tool for diffusing the urge to indulge your out-of-control behavior, and this is the topic of today's stopping lesson. Tomorrow's lesson builds on how to use peace to access wisdom and strength from your Christ-self by dismantling the ego pattern-repeating robot that lives in you.

Peace is one of those things everyone says they want. *Rah, rah peace.* That is, until it comes to doing the work of cultivating a peaceful state of mind. Then the desire for peace goes out the window and excitement or distraction is craved. You probably already noticed a resistance to doing your daily meditation practice and a secret preference for doing anything other than sitting still. This preference is your first obstacle to peace. Very few people like sitting still and even fewer believe that *doing nothing* is useful or that it solves problems.

Think of how you approach problem-solving in your own life. There's always an action involved. *What are you going to do about it?* Americans, especially, are trained to *do something* about every unwanted condition or emotion. How can *doing nothing* actually work? How can it possibly be the smartest choice when *doing something* is so much more appealing and satisfying? The thing to keep in mind is that you're not being asked to do nothing forever. Doing nothing is your immediate response to any provocation. This doesn't mean you never do anything. It does mean that you do nothing until the provocation of the moment passes. It's always the wisest, smartest and most harmless choice. Here's a real life example that demonstrates how doing nothing works to end provocation.

Last summer my husband and I vacationed on the Outer Banks of North Carolina, a beautiful part of the country we'd never visited before. The extreme heat and the novelty of renting a beach house with five other families, all relatives, makes this vacation stand out as a memorable event. Afternoons often included a cooling jump in the pool to take a respite from the sweltering heat. One day one of the kids decided to make a little mischief by shooting water bombs at the people congregating in the pool. He had a giant-sized plastic water pump gun, the kind that can really do a formidable job of getting you drenched. Most of us put up a good defense, which included splashing back, squealing, pleading with the kid to stop, and chasing him, but one of my cousins had a different and better response. She didn't yell at the kid. She didn't beg him to stop. She didn't yip or squeal. Instead, she turned around and let the kid shoot as much water as he wanted at her back. All it took was one lowly minute for the kid to be totally bored and to stop tormenting my cousin.

Those of us who responded to the water bomb torment got more water bomb torment. The one who didn't respond got less torment. More accurately, ultimately she ended the torment and made it stop. The big secret that no one else will tell you is that responding to tension brings more tension. Not responding to tension ends it. Tension passes, *on its own*, without doing anything. Doing nothing is peace.

When you *do something* to indulge your unwanted behavior, you are not releasing, diffusing or neutralizing your inner tension. The tension is still there, deep inside you, but it's temporarily sedated. Sedation makes you feel like you're relaxed and worry-free, but it's a temporary kind of relaxation that cannot be relied upon. After the sedation wears off, your impulsive tension pops out again, stronger than ever. The brief moments of relief you give yourself allow you to escape from your tension without actually resolving it. The only long term, permanent resolution for impulsive tension is to stop responding to it. When you stop responding, something strange happens because you start wondering if your impulsive tension is real. Treating your impulsive tension like it's nothing, opens the door to actually thinking it's nothing, and this is truly a revolutionary thought.

The physical experience of dealing with impulsive tension is very much like the experience of doing an unfamiliar stretching-type exercise or a new yoga pose. The first time you do the stretch, you notice a pinched or strained feeling in the part of your body that you're working. The tense discomfort is your own resistance to the stretching experience. Once you stop resisting the pose and relax into it, the strained feeling starts dissipating. The longer you hold the pose, the less you feel the strain or tension. Usually, all it takes is about 30 seconds or so for the tension to lessen. If you work with the same stretch for a few days or a week or two, a day comes when you don't feel the tension at all. It's gone. Done. There is no tension. Tension from your unwanted behavior is minimized or eliminated by holding it and relaxing into it, too.

Release your tension by allowing it to be expressed and to run its course, but without responding to it. Everything inside you might be screaming to *do something* to get rid of the yukky tense feeling, but instead of reacting to the tension, *you choose to do nothing*. You're at peace with it. You let it be. Yes, just like a new stretch, it's temporarily uncomfortable to hold your tension, but it's not unbearable or excruciatingly painful. And yes, just like a new stretch, your tension disappears in a relatively short period of time. Minutes, not hours. Days, not years. As you consistently and repetitively stop responding to your impulsive tension, gradually it becomes less and less intense. The more you continue to hold your peace, the more your tension gets diffused. The reservoir of tension that's been inside you dries up. One day the intensity is so minor that you don't even notice it. Then, voila, there is no tension. It's gone. Done.

We have not been taught to hold our tension. Bodily urges are much more likely to be honored and revered rather than over-ridden or transcended. *That pesky urge must mean something psychologically or emotionally important, right?* But it isn't anything important. It's just the same old urge to self-destruct that everyone has, and self-destruction is a meaningless waste. Do your best to withdraw all honor and importance from your self-destructive urges. They're not worthy of your attention. They deserve to be overlooked and treated like nothing.

Holding tension is sometimes mistakenly perceived as an act of repression or denial. This is not a correct or accurate perception because you're not denying the impulsive tension or pretending it's not there. Rather, you're acknowledging your tension, you're fully accepting it, and you're allowing it to be experienced. Then you're deliberately and consciously choosing not to respond to it. This is the important part, and this is the difference! Contrary to popular opinion, intentionally holding on to your impulsive tension is not dangerous. It will not hurt or kill you. It doesn't make you dysfunctional. It doesn't make you angry or frustrated. It doesn't have to have any negative effect on you whatsoever. Until now, you haven't been exposed to the concept of holding onto impulsive tension. You haven't been trained to do it. And you haven't understood the benefit of doing it. You are just now on the cusp of understanding.

Part of that understanding is the recognition that you're walking with the Christ, not with other egos. Consequently, don't expect to get social reinforcement or social recognition for using peace as your stopping tool. No attention is drawn to self. No one comes up to you and holds your hand. No one pats you on your back and tells you how noble or great you are. There are no whistles and bells with peace.

No one realizes that peace is an active, conscious choice that requires effort on your part. It is not a special experience. Prepare for this non-experience. Expect it.

When you're at peace, you're aligning with the Christ, and the Christ is very quiet.

DAY 12 STOPPING PRACTICE

MIND: The skill of the mind is to make a decision and hold it.

1. Slowly write out your stopping intention eight times.
2. Slowly say your intention out loud eight times in front of a mirror.
3. Create a 2nd rejection visualization using a different scene. Follow the same three-scene process but change the place and timing where you reject your favored substance. Be sure to end with a visual image of yourself smiling.

SPIRIT: The skill of the spirit is to experience an instant of inner peace so that you can turn off the ego and connect with your Christ self.

Your meditation period is the practical, learn-by-doing methodology for training yourself to have the experience of peace. Unwanted behaviors cannot be undone when emotional turmoil or panic disturbs your mind. A calm experience in the mind is essential for a calm experience in your body, and this is what you are giving yourself. It only *seems* like nothing is happening.

Today's practice is two 7-minute minute meditation periods. Do your first meditation early in the morning, as soon as practical. Do the second one whenever it's convenient. Use the meditation phrase as much as you can throughout the day, at least 24 times, which is roughly once every half hour. You can't overdo it.

Today's meditation phrase

I want the peace of God.

HEART: The skill of the heart is to make self happy. Your happiness is the most important thing in the world and cannot be sacrificed for any reason.

Write out your life purpose statement. Make your writing an act of love.

Draw a picture of your happiness. *(Stick figures are fine.)*

Briefly describe how your life purpose has the potential to change your life.

BODY: The skill of the body is to use physical tension to diffuse physical tension.

Type exercise: Aerobics

Activity: <u>Brisk</u> walking

Time: 15 <u>continuous</u> minutes

Pedometer people. Add another 250 steps today. This is +1,000 steps from your starting point. At the end of the day, record the total number of steps you took in your *Miracle Stopping Journal.*

As always, comment about your activity experience.

MORE POWER SKILL OF THE SPIRIT

Peace dismantles the ego pattern-repeating robot

It is through the holy instant that what seems to be impossible
is accomplished, making it evident that it is not impossible.

A COURSE IN MIRACLES

Everyone has had the experience of driving a car and somehow ending up at the intended destination, but without a clue how you got there. You can thank your ego robot for this mysterious, zombie-like phenomenon. Your ego robot takes over for you and makes it possible to go through the motions of life, mindlessly, without awareness of what you're doing and without paying attention to what you're doing. From a metaphysical perspective, mindless and robotic behavior is the experience of separation. Separation occurs because you're alienated from the present moment. Instead of *being there*, you can sneak away and daydream, worry, multi-task or zone out. Whenever you do anything on *automatic* your ego robot is in control.

A robot is an artificial intelligence machine that does things for you, and the ego robot is no exception. It's an intelligent machine that takes over and does all the dull, repetitive tasks of living. In fact, if you allow it, your ego robot exempts you from having to *be there* to do anything and everything. God knows, we humans are very attached to our labor-saving devices. We love being freed from the work that machines do for us. We love the ease and convenience. We love saving time. Why bother with all the mechanical and mundane life tasks when you have a willing and able ego to do the grunt work you? Robots are usually perceived as friendly, harmless and sometimes comical devices that do your bidding and make your life better. Unfortunately, the ego robot is not friendly because it turns you into a mindless, pattern-repeating machine. You never have to pay attention to what you're doing. You never have to make the acts you perform in your life count. You never have to make yourself happy by doing something creative or meaningful. It's possible to shuffle through life without ever having to think very much about what you're doing. When your actions are dominated by one mechanical, soulless process after another, life does not satisfy. It's worth remembering that a pattern *is not conscious thinking*. It's just a stream of actions that are tacked together in a very specific programmed order. When you're in your pattern, you're in a trance. You're not paying attention. You're not aware. You're just going through motions.

Being a machine, the ego performs the same identical sequential motions over and over again. This is the ego's strength, and it's also the ego's weakness. All machines have a standard process or a fixed set of steps that <u>must</u> be followed. Otherwise, the machine doesn't work. Think of the fixed set of steps that you have to follow to access email on your computer. First you have to make sure that the computer has power. Then you have to make sure that it's connected to the internet. Then you have to make sure your email app is up and running. Then you have to make sure your email account is set up correctly. Then you have to press send/receive to get your mail. This is a lot of steps that you don't even think about. If one of the steps doesn't work, you won't be able to get your email, and you'll have to troubleshoot where the problem is.

All machines depend on an <u>exact</u> pattern sequence, including the ego pattern-repeating machine. The good news is that all you have to do is dismantle one simple step to screw up the mechanical process. One small disruption in the sequence makes the machine dysfunctional or it makes it stop working altogether, and this is what you're after. A machine is not creative, and it cannot spontaneously fix a malfunction. This is why, mechanically speaking, it's very easy to stop yourself. One little disruption is all it takes. Really, that's it. The tool for creating the disruption is a moment of peace. *A Course In Miracles* calls this brief moment of peace the Holy Instant. It's holy because you're temporarily turning off your ego.

Whenever you turn off, transcend or override the ego, even if it's just the briefest moment, your Christ-self <u>must</u> come through. It cannot be avoided. Your mind has only two channels: the ego and your Christ-self. When the ego is turned off, the Christ-self is automatically present. The thing to keep in mind is that this is a *subtle* and unexciting connection. The Christ in you is still and quiet. Chances are, you're not going to hear a voice that says, *Yo dude, Jesus of Nazareth here.* And you're not going to feel transported to heaven, either. What you feel is very aware and very alive. That's all. There's no drama. No flood of emotion. No excitement.

Whenever the impulse to use the substance or engage in the unwanted behavior presents itself, use this *Prayer of the Holy Instant* to pause your action, override your ego and put you in connection with your Source of power, the Christ-self.

This is my holy instant of release.
I can feel peace instead of this.
I ask the Christ to fill me with
His strength, His peace and His resolve.

Can you hold your peace for an instant? All you ever need is one Holy Instant. The Holy Instant puts you in the realm of miracles where the laws of the physical world are reversed and where weakness is transmuted into strength.

Even though the Christ that dwells within is immutable and strong, your connection to the Christ is still weak because you haven't used it. Luckily, you can quickly make your connection strong again. Spiritual fitness works just like physical fitness. Muscles in your body need to be systematically trained and conditioned to look better and function better. Imagine, for example, how toned your biceps would look and how well they would perform if you lifted 20-pound barbells ten times every day for the last ten years? Now imagine how flabby and weak your biceps would be if you never lifted anything over the same period of time.

From this point forward, you'll be developing your connecting link to your Christ-self through the exercise of daily communion. The purpose of communion is to develop your strength, to access your own wisdom, and to come to rely on the Christ as a resource in solving problems and navigating through life.

> *The sight of Christ is all there is to see.*
> *The song of Christ is all there is to hear.*
> *The hand of Christ is all there is to hold.*
> *There is no journey but to walk with Him.*

DAY 13 STOPPING PRACTICE

MIND: The skill of the mind is to make a decision and hold it.

1. Write your intention statement in long-hand 10 times.

2. Say your intention out loud 10 times in front of a mirror.

3. Play your 2nd rejection visualization in your mind 3 times

SPIRIT: The skill of the spirit is to experience an instant of inner peace so that you can turn off the ego and connect with your sacred power.

Today's meditation phrase

Memorize and recite your Holy Instant prayer:

> *This is my holy instant of release.*
> *I can feel peace instead of this.*
> *I ask the Christ to fill me with*
> *His strength, His peace and His resolve.*

Practice saying the phrase over and over for 5 minutes or as long as you need. Then say the prayer once an hour throughout the day, more often if you need it. Keep track of your practice performance in your *Miracle Stopping Journal.*

Right after your five-minute meditation period, sit in silence for another minute or two. When you're completely relaxed, ask the following question in your mind.

Repeat it two or three times until the question is anchored. Then sit still and let the answer come to you. It may take another minute or two. Try to maintain your meditative state of mind as you capture your response in your *Miracle Stopping Journal.*

Communion question

Teacher, what does my father will me to know about stopping myself?

NOTE: I use the terms *father* and *he* in communion exercises. If these gender terms don't feel comfortable to you, substitute any others that work better for you. Also, while it's possible that some people will actually hear a Voice, it's much more likely that you'll have a very clear, very sure, very loving thought. If you don't get an answer after a few minutes, don't worry. It's your own resistance holding it back. The answer will come to you in a moment of unguarded relaxation, like when you're in the shower or loading the dishwasher. Trust that if you ask the question, the answer will come.

HEART: The skill of the heart is to make self happy. Your happiness is the most important thing in the world and cannot be sacrificed for any reason.

Answer these questions

1. What makes you laugh out loud really hard?
2. Try to make yourself laugh out loud really hard, right now.
3. What can you do to experience more laughter in your life?

BODY: The skill of the body is to use physical tension to diffuse physical tension.

Go to www.powertostop.com/tools for instruction, if needed.

Type Exercise:	Flexibility
Activity:	Stretching of all major joints

Time: 10 Minutes (more is okay)

Pedometer people: Add another 250 steps today. This is a total of + 1,250 steps from your starting point. At the end of the day, record your actual step performance in your *Miracle Stopping Journal.*

Write about your exercise experience. Explain when, where, and how it felt.

Day 14

REVIEW OF WEEK TWO

Think about the kind of day you want, and tell yourself there
is a way in which this very day can happen just like that.

A COURSE IN MIRACLES

As you already know, reviews are designed to reinforce and consolidate the ideas presented in the previous week.

Week two accomplishments

♥ You progressively increased the four stopping skills that enable you to stop yourself.

♥ You learned how to construct and use a visualization technique for rejecting your unwanted behavior.

♥ You made a first pass at figuring out your life purpose and you identified activities that make you happy.

♥ You have a more thorough understanding of peace and why it's an effective stopping tool.

♥ You re-examined concepts involving boundaries, specialness and disease.

Which weekly activity was most helpful to you?

DAY 14 STOPPING PRACTICE

MIND: The skill of the mind is to make a decision and hold it.

1. Write out your stopping intention. Self-determine how many times you should repeat the writing exercise.

2. Say your stopping intention out loud in front of a mirror. Self-determine how many times you recite it.

3. Play your visualization exercise in your mind. Self-determine how many times you should repeat the visualization.

Are you satisfied with your intention statement and visualizations? Is there something you can do to enhance your *say it, see it* exercises to make them stronger, fresher and more inspiring?

SPIRIT: The skill of the spirit is to experience an instant of inner peace so that you can turn off the ego and connect with your Christ self.

Read the six meditation phrases that were provided during your second week. Pick the one that's most meaningful for you, follow the time directions associated with the phrase, and use it for your meditation today.

Write this phrase in your *Miracle Stopping Journal* and explain why it's important to you.

HEART: The skill of the heart is to make self happy. Your happiness is the most important thing in the world and cannot be sacrificed for any reason.

Write out your life purpose statement. Set your timer for two minutes. Brainstorm all the things you can do to manifest your life mission and make it a tangible, ordinary, everyday experience. Don't judge your responses. Just write, unstopped, for two full minutes.

BODY: The skill of the body is to use physical tension to diffuse physical tension.

This is a physical rest day. No activity is required.

Summarize your weekly exercise experience. Note the increase in time and the type of exercise you most prefer.

RATE YOUR 2nd WEEK:

Use a scale of (1) low to (10) high. Rate your weekly experience on the program, and briefly explain why you gave this rating.

What are you doing well?

What can you do better?

Day 15

THE POWER SKILL OF THE MIND

Set your intention

This is why the question, "what do you want?" must be
answered. You are answering it every minute and every second..
Its effects will follow automatically until the decision is made.

A COURSE IN MIRACLES

I s getting what you want a random process, like haphazardly pulling petals off a
daisy? Why do you sometimes get what you want and other times you don't? Is
God making a decision about whether you can have it or not? For sure, worthiness
is a relevant factor, but it's not God who's judging you as worthy. It's you. You're
the judge and jury of your life performance, which is why you must increase your
perception of your own worthiness. A tool for doing this is provided later this week.
Today's lesson is about knowing what you want, the other key factor that enables
you to manifest your desires. To get what you want you have to know what you
want, and you have to know it with 100% sureness.

The moment your desire is clearly identified, you intuitively and automatically start moving toward it. In fact, once you know what you want and you're 100% sure about it, it's hard to stop yourself from getting it. You decide your house needs to be cleaned, and before you know it the Pledge is in your hand and you're cleaning like crazy. You decide you need a new winter coat, and soon after you make the decision, you go out shopping and buy one. You decide you need a new haircut, and in a week or two your hair is shorter. You decide you need a new lover, and voila, you start pulling yourself together, and before you know it you have a new love interest. There's nothing complicated or unusual about knowing what you want and getting it for yourself. You do it all the time without instruction or reminders from anyone.

Every kind of desire is automatically fulfilled, and this is true whether the desire is noble or ignoble, conscious or unconscious. The trick with wanting something is to want it consciously because then all those ignoble desires can be overridden. Conscious desires are the ones that are in alignment with your Christ-self. Unconscious desires are the ones that aren't in alignment with your Christ-self. We've already talked about how garbage ego thoughts predominate in the untrained mind. This means that garbage unconscious desires also predominate in the mind. The purpose of using a daily intention statement is to have a systematic, disciplined process for training your mind so that your conscious desires cut through all this confusion and dominate over unconscious ones. Without this process (or another one like it), your unconscious desires will go unchecked, and they will continue to direct you.

The rule for overriding distracting ego thoughts and desires is to pay attention to what you want and to ignore what you don't want. Easy to talk about, harder to do. Hateful, fearful, destructive thoughts show up in your mind, and the great temptation for everyone is to indulge these thoughts by paying attention to them and by allowing them to distract you. The impulse to self-destruct is an example of a hateful, fearful thought that takes up a lot of real estate in your mind and seems true. So what are you going to do when the idea pops up? Do you continue to respond to it and give it a place of honor in your life? Or will you change your mind by changing your thought?

Obviously, the goal here is to change your mind. The very minute you become aware of the destructive thought, swap it out with your stopping intention. Fortunately, the mind can only hold one thought at a time. Your intention serves you in two ways: 1) by changing your mind about what you want, and 2) by uplifting your mind out of a dark place and into a light one. That's a bona fide two-fer! You've been making the same straightforward, unambiguous stopping intention since Day 1 of the *Power to Stop* Program. This puts you way ahead in the stopping game. Your daily skill of the mind practice builds on your stopping intention to make it a strong, unimpeachable and resolute thought. You are, after all, the only one who has to be convinced and trained to believe in your intention.

Here are ten ridiculously easy guidelines for constructing and using stopping intentions as you go forward. You should recognize many of them.

1. Your stopping intention is a positive description of the result you want to achieve. Do your very best not to reinforce or give attention to the behavior that isn't wanted. As you now know, this takes a little extra awareness and effort.

2. Construct your intention using words that are personally meaningful, exciting and inspiring. Change the words as soon as they get stale or boring.

3. Express your intention in the present tense, *as if* it's happening now.

4. Keep it short and easy to memorize.

5. Use the pronoun "I" or your first name.

6. Express your intention in three ways: in writing, vocally and by making a picture of it in your mind.

7. Your intention is an act of creation, and as such, it deserves your respect. Express it calmly and slowly, without any sense of rush. Try your best not to turn your intention exercise into a mindless ritual that's quickly rattled off.

8. Once a week treat your intention as a daily meditation exercise, where you repeat the same thought over and over, consistently for 5 or 10 minutes.

9. Stand in front of a mirror and watch yourself recite your intention out loud.

10. Repeat your intention every morning and multiple times throughout the day.

There are three tried and true, highly effective techniques for religiously reminding yourself to repeat your intention during the day. The first is to link your recitations to pre-existing daily routines like drinking coffee in the morning, showering, mealtimes, and driving. These are easy, built-in prompts that trigger you to state your intention. The second technique is to use a counting tool. This could be rosary or prayer beads, dried beans in a container, or tick marks on your daily to do list. The third technique is to use a timing device like your smart phone or your watch to give you a series of reminder alarms throughout the day. Experiment with the techniques, then pick the one you like best and use it.

You are a magnificent creator, and you create the life experience you want through your desire, which is expressed as an intention statement. Your intention creates all financial success, all relationship success, all spiritual success, all academic success, and all stopping success. Everything you achieve comes from your intention to achieve it. Once you make the conscious decision and set your intention, the rest is pretty darn easy. The hard part is firmly making the decision about what you want. This is where most people freeze up or get confused, and this is where problems crop up. If you're having trouble implementing your intention to stop, or if you're stopping and going, then look right here at the firmness of your decision. It needs more work.

An unclear, infirm stopping intention leads to unclear, infirm stopping results. Comments like the ones that follow came up in the very first stopping seminar I ever conducted over 20 years ago, and they're still coming up today. Invariably, someone says *I don't know for sure if I want to stop, I just want to like myself better. Or, I'd like to accept myself as I am, without stopping, and be happy about it.* When the intention to stop isn't clear and firm, behavior always defaults and falls back to the easier position of not stopping self. We've already talked about the link between wasting your life and unhappiness, and this is still the strongest case for making a firm no decision.

You already made your decision, and your response to the Call of Love is now in your heart – forever. It cannot be undone. I might have forgotten to mention this to you. So, in a sense, you're stuck with your decision to heal and to become whole. There's really no going back. If you're struggling, you have the dilemma of perhaps not fully wanting to go forward, either. The smartest way to deal with your struggle is to end the conflict and stop struggling. Accept you are a warrior and this is your life path. Accept the sensations in your body are your own precious life force. Accept that you're a hard nut to crack and that you have to keep intending the same stopping decision. Maybe you have to intend it 1,000 times. Maybe it's 2,000. Maybe it's 20,000. You are so worth the effort.

The big question everyone wants to know is how long it takes to manifest the intention. Think of each repetition of your intention statement as a boiling hot drop of water that you put into a tub that's filled with ice cubes. First you have to generate enough boiling hot drops of water to melt the cubes of ice. Then you have to keep generating enough boiling hot drops to turn frigid cold water into warm water. So how long does it take to get the water warm enough to manifest your intention? Like everything, this is up to you. How much do you want it? How much attention and energy do you bring to training your mind? How consistent are you?

Continue with your daily stopping intention activities whether you've completely stopped yourself or not. Putting your intention out into the universe works the same as putting a sail out into the wind to capture energy. The wind might not be there right away, but sooner or later it comes along, fills the sail, and takes you where you want to go. In the meantime, keep your sail out. Do your daily intention work, no matter what. Yes, it's repetitious. Yes, it can be boring, but it works. Make the process as interesting and as lively as you can make it, and wait patiently for the universal wind of inspiration to catch you because it will.

DAY 15 STOPPING PRACTICE

MIND: The skill of the mind is to make a decision and hold it.

1. Write out your stopping intention three times. At the end of the statement, add *God is the strength in which <u>I trust.</u> I give my intention to my Christ-self to fulfill.*

2. Say your stopping intention out loud three times. Do it with attitude. Add pauses, exclamations, silliness or drama.

3. Pick one of your visualization exercises and play it in your mind three times.

4. Decide what kind of day you want for yourself. Then ask your Christ-self to give it to you.

SPIRIT: The skill of the spirit is to experience an instant of inner peace so that you can turn off the ego and connect with your Christ self.

Today's goal is a total of 13 minutes of meditation. Do one 10-minute meditation period in the morning and another 3-minute meditation period later in the day, whenever it's convenient. Recite the meditation phrase 12 times throughout the day, which is approximately one each hour. Do your communion exercise after one of your meditation periods, when your mind is still.

Today's meditation phrase

My Father gives all power unto me. There is no limit on my strength.

Communion question

Teacher, what does my Father Will me to know about His strength that is available to me?

Remember to capture your response in your *Miracle Stopping Journal*.

HEART: The skill of the heart is to make self happy. Your happiness is the most important thing in the world and cannot be sacrificed for any reason.

Write out your life purpose statement. Yesterday you brainstormed a list of activities that you can do to manifest your purpose. Look at your list and pick one activity. Figure out how to incorporate this activity into your life.

What are you going to do?
When are you going to do it?
How will you do it?

Write you plan in your *Miracle Stopping Journal.*

BODY: The skill of the body is to use physical tension to diffuse physical tension.

This week you'll be mildly increasing the time and intensity of your exercise sessions so that you get a bigger and more effective relaxation response. Here's a summary of your weekly activity schedule:

Day 15	*Day 16*	*Day 17*	*Day 18*	*Day 19*	*Day 20*	*Day 21*
Aerobic	*Strength*	*Aerobic*	*Strength*	*Aerobic*	*Flexibility*	*Off*

Today's exercise: Aerobic

Activity: Brisk walking with five 1-minute intervals of light jogging

See below for minute-by-minute walk/jog guidelines

Time: 20 minutes

Minutes 1-4	Brisk Walking
Minute 5	Light Jogging
Minute 6-7	Brisk Walking

Minute 8	Light Jogging
Minute 9-10	Brisk Walking
Minute 11	Light Jogging
Minute 12-13	Brisk Walking
Minute 14	Light Jogging
Minute 15-16	Brisk Walking
Minute 17	Light Jogging
Minute 18-20	Brisk Walking

Pedometer people: Add 250 steps today. This is a total of + 1,500 from your starting point.

As always, write about your exercise experience. Notice and comment on what happens when you add intensity, if anything.

Day 16
MORE POWER SKILL OF THE MIND
Hold your intention

What you do comes from what you think.
A COURSE IN MIRACLES

I t's one thing to want to stop yourself when the goal of stopping is like a hot poker in your mind, and it's quite another thing to keep your stopping desire alive over a long period of time, after the heat of the moment has passed. Life is very interesting and intoxicating. There are many other things to want along the way, and there are many distractions to occupy your mind. Making money, spending money. Finding love, making love. Family activities, family problems. Household chores, goofing off. Everything is competing for your attention at the same time. Absorption in the distractions of life seduces you into forgetting your stopping goal. When people don't succeed in stopping, it's because they forgot their intention before it was firm and unshakeable.

Concentration is the art of holding your intention in the forefront of your mind until it gets firm and strong. You'll know when your intention is strong because you're 100% sure about it, and there's no doubt or conflict in your mind about your ability to stop yourself. When this happens, you no longer need your intention statement. It takes a little while for this kind of strength of mind to develop. Be patient with yourself. Think of your intention as a little seed that you plant in the ground. It takes a week of two for the seed to germinate. Then it takes another week or so before it breaks through the ground and turns into a seedling. And then it takes another two or three weeks before the seedling gets strong enough to make it through all the challenges that life presents. Keep repeating your intention until it germinates, sprouts and gets strong. There's no exact science about how much time it takes, but plan on nurturing your intention for the full 30 day program period and perhaps longer.

The practice of concentrating on your intention, and repeating it over and over is an ancient practice used by many formal religions and mind-training systems.

> After studying the various mystical religions and different teachings and systems of mind-stuff, I'm impressed that they all have the same basic modus operandi. That is, they achieve success through repetition – the repeating of certain mantras, words or formulas.... One finds the same principle at work in chants, incantations, litanies, daily lessons (to be repeated as frequently as possible during the week), and the frequent praying of Buddhists and Moslems alike.
>
> Claude M. Bristol
> **THE MAGIC OF BELIEVING**

Your intention statement is your handy tool for concentrating your thinking. Concentration is desirable because it's more powerful than thoughts that are diffused or erratic. The problem with concentrated thinking is that it's sometimes confused with obsessive thinking. There's a very fine line between concentrating on something and obsessing over it. Both types of thoughts guide you, so in a way, obsessive thinking works. The difference is that obsessive thinking ultimately leads to harmfulness, and concentrated thinking does not. Obsessive thinking is frantic; concentration is calm. When you're obsessing, you end up making that *no matter what it takes* choice to get it. It's an over-zealous emphasis on *getting* the result. Happiness along the way doesn't matter. Kindness to self or others along the way doesn't matter. Going with God along the way doesn't matter. The only thing that matters is getting the thing you want so you can be happy later, when you get it.

Obsession crops up as a problem for people who tack a secondary goal onto their stopping objective. A stopping goal, for example, might be linked to the restoration of a relationship goal. Or it might be linked to a better career goal. In particular, people who have the goal of stopping self from over eating almost always have a dual, simultaneous goal of losing weight. Obsession relates to the level of intensity or effort that you put into achieving your goals. It's the idea that if a little effort is good, a lot more effort is better. Pushing and straining are clues that you're rejecting your current experience. You don't want what's happening now; you want something better in the future. It's a fearful experience because you're secretly worried if you don't *go fast and get it over with*, you might not be able to hold your intention and get what you want. So you push and you hurry yourself to make the result come sooner.

Too much effort is like too much fertilizer on a plant. Excuse the constant plant analogies. It comes with being a gardener. When you give a plant the appropriate amount of fertilizer, it grows. When you give a plant too much fertilizer, the plant gets overwhelmed by the extra energy, and it can't handle it. Pretty soon the leaves start to burn and fall off, the plant weakens, and eventually the plant might even die. You can't handle extra energy all at once, either. You will kill your intention seedling when you over fertilize it.

The Japanese call this kind of over-the-top energy *faido*, and it always works against you. There's no word for it in English, but faido exists. Prevent faido by letting your secondary result go, for now, and focusing on your primary goal of stopping. Stopping by itself is much easier than stopping plus trying to do something else at the same time. Stopping is what's most important. This is what you're here for. Sure, it's okay to have secondary goals, but keep them in second place and hold them lightly. Don't get confused or crazy with other intentions. Accept the slow, plodding speed that comes with stopping yourself and refuse to rush or push so you can get onto the next thing. Instead of lusting for future happiness, be happy now by going fully into the stopping experience. Give yourself to it.

Concentration is more efficient than obsession because the energy pattern is firm, straight and strong, like a laser beam of light. The stronger your intention, the thicker the beam of light, and the easier it is to hit the target. Obsession has a different look. In some places it's thick, in other places it's wispy, and there are a lot of spikes and dips. The spikes and dips are surges of excess energy that take you off track and that unnecessarily use up a lot of your power. What good have you done for yourself if you expend all your effort in a few days and burn yourself out? What good have you done for yourself if you use up all your energy setting your intention and have nothing left for the hard work of maintaining it? No good comes to you from obsessing. All good comes to you by calmly and steadily holding your intention in the forefront of your mind. Rushing and pushing is risky business. Why bother with it?

Your intention is to your mind as what gas is to a car.

♥ When you put a little trickle of gas in your car, you might be able to drive a block or two, but not much farther. When you trickle a few intentions in your mind, you might last a day or two.

♥ When you fill your car tank once and forget about it, you might be able to travel 200 or 300 miles, which is a great start, but after that you'll be stranded. When you fill your mind with intentions for a week and then forget about them, you'll get off to a solid start, and then you'll stall.

♥ What you need is an ongoing supply of gas for as long as you want to drive the car. Your daily intention work is your stopping fuel.

Keep your mind tank filled with your intention until you reach your destination.

DAY 16 STOPPING PRACTICE

MIND: The skill of the mind is to make a decision and hold it.

Prevent boredom, staleness and mindless robotic actions with small, frequent changes to your stopping intention and by expressing your intention in lively, interesting ways. This keeps the experience fresh and exciting. Without these small periodic modifications, you risk getting bored with the process.

1. If you feel it's necessary, brainstorm a new stopping intention for yourself.

2. Write out your stopping intention three times. At the end of your statement, add *God is the strength in which I follow. I give my intention to my Christ-self to fulfill.*

3. Say your intention out loud in three different ways. Say it fast. Say it slow. Say it with exaggerated enunciation on each word.

4. Decide what kind of day you want it to be. Ask your Christ-self to give it to you.

SPIRIT: The skill of the spirit is to experience an instant of inner peace so that you can turn off the ego and connect with your Christ self.

Your goal for today is a total of 14 minutes of meditation time. Do one long 9-minute meditation period at the start of the day and a shorter 5-minute meditation period later on, whenever it's convenient for you. Recite your meditation phrase at meal times and before you go to bed. Your communion exercise should be done immediately after your long meditation period, when your mind is peaceful and relaxed.

Today's meditation phrase

I rule my mind, which I alone must rule.

Communion question

Teacher, what does my Father Will me to know about my purpose?

Remember to capture your response in your *Miracle Stopping Journal.*

HEART: The skill of the heart is to make self happy. Your happiness is the most important thing in the world and cannot be sacrificed for any reason.

Answer this series of questions

1. How do you recognize if someone in your world is happy or not?

2. Why do you think this person so happy?

3. Who is this person, and what happiness techniques can you copy from him/her?

BODY: The skill of the body is to use physical tension to diffuse physical tension.

Today is a strength training day. The objective with strength training is to *fatigue* or tire the muscle group you're working, and this is done by adding intensity to your moves. It's accomplished either by adding weights, by doing more repetitions or by holding an isometric pose for 10 seconds or more. If you have the time and the financial means, consider joining a health club that has a circuit of weight training machines because a weight-training circuit is the fastest, safest and most efficient way to fatigue and condition your muscles. A health club environment also provides you with a place and a structured format for continuing to take care of your body in a way that results in a rapid and powerful relaxation response.

If you're working out at home and need direction, go to <u>www.powertostop.com/tools</u> for strength-training instruction.

Type exercise:	Strength Conditioning
Activity:	Calisthenics at home, a DVD workout, or weight training on a machine circuit at a health club
Time:	20 minutes minimum
	Warm-up

- 5 minutes of abdominal work

- 5 minutes of upper body work

- 10 minutes of lower body work

Pedometer people: Add another 250 steps today. This is a total of + 1,750 from your starting point. At the end of the day, record the actual number of steps you took in your *Miracle Stopping Journal.*

As always, write about your exercise experience. Notice and comment on what happens when you add intensity, if anything.

THE POWER SKILL OF THE HEART

*Disconnection makes you unhappy and
social forgiveness is disconnection.*

The ego's plan for forgiveness is far more widely used than God's.
A COURSE IN MIRACLES

A ll happiness comes from meaningful connection. The happiest people are the most connected people. The unhappiest people are the ones who are most disconnected and separate. This is why solitary confinement in prison is the most extreme form of punishment. Separation is the worst feeling in the world. In fact, it's the experience of hell. Since the power skill of the heart is to make yourself happy, connecting will be a constant feature in your life.

Connection is defined as relationship or joining, and there are several important and different ways to do it. We've already discussed *connecting* to the present moment, *connecting* to your own aliveness and life energy, *connecting* to your passion and purpose, and *connecting* to God and your Christ-self. Today's stopping lesson is about strengthening your connection to others. As you already know, relationships with others can be a bittersweet combination of bliss and torment. The bliss part happens when you're in sync with the people in your world. The torment part happens when you're out of sync or in conflict. Sometimes being out of sync is so distracting and so troubling, it makes it hard to function normally. This, of course, makes it doubly hard to stop yourself or to stay stopped. Who cares about stopping when the pain of separation is on your mind and in your face? This is why bringing peace to your relationships is a practical and important stopping strategy. You don't have to go back into your past to find peace with your relationships. It's all done in the present moment, as upsets are remembered or as new ones crop up. Peaceful relationships with others are a key to your happiness.

Peace is always disrupted when you *indulge* your hateful thoughts about yourself or another. As we've already discussed, hateful, destructive thoughts appear in everyone's mind, but they don't have to be believed, kept or treated as important. Guilt is a hateful, destructive thought turned inward on self. Anger is a hateful, destructive thought extended outwards towards another. Both are equally unsettling and distracting, so one is not better or less objectionable than another. That said, many people mistakenly perceive guilt as more okay than anger. A little guilt is valued because it *supposedly* inspires correction and becoming a better person. This is an example of the massive public misperception that guilt and correction are the same. Guilt is a form of hate in the mind, and correction is fixing an error. These are two wildly different concepts. Correction can and does occur without guilt.

Angry, guilty thoughts are both undone in the same way: by exchanging a hateful thought for a neutral or positive one. No one likes to believe it's this astoundingly simple, but it is. We'd rather have steps, counseling, letter writing that says we *might* forgive someday (but not now), preparation rituals of every kind, long periods of hurt feelings, emotional confrontations, pills for coping and whatever else you can conjure up to delay real forgiveness. Forget all that stuff. You can do it if you want, but it's not necessary. None of it. All that's really required is that you change your mind. We talked about the fact that the mind can only hold one thought at a time, so having a neutral or positive thought bumps out a hateful one. Whenever you replace your hateful thought with a harmless one, you experience yourself as love.

The fastest, most efficient way to change a hateful thought to a loving one is through the deliberate, conscious practice of forgiveness. Okay, I know. Forgiveness has a very bad rap. Before you get all worked up about being asked to forgive yourself or another, please know there are two versions of forgiveness. There's social forgiveness, which is the version of forgiveness you're already familiar with, and there's the spiritual forgiveness, which is the version of forgiveness that will be new to you. Spiritual forgiveness is the topic of tomorrow's lesson. The only thing that social forgiveness and spiritual forgiveness have in common is the term *forgiveness*. Everything else is completely different.

Social forgiveness is *fake* forgiveness. Instead of neutralizing or undoing the underlying hateful thought, social forgiveness extends hate and keeps it alive. In contrast, the one and only goal of spiritual forgiveness is to transcend hate and to undo the hateful thought. Hateful thoughts create distance, and in case you haven't noticed, distance is the opposite of joining and connection. When you're angry with another, you don't want to be with this person. You want to reject, get away and be separate. Guilty thoughts create distance and separation, too. Whenever you feel guilty, you want to shrink yourself and contract so that no one sees you or interacts with you. Anger and guilt both exacerbate the impulse to self-destruct, and this is why *a little* anger or guilt is never desirable or helpful.

Social forgiveness keeps anger and guilt alive for as long as possible. This is the primary reason it should be reconsidered for what it is: a set of conventions or unwritten rules that we all *agree* to follow. Here are the six most common conventions for fake, social forgiveness.

> *Convention #1:* The person to be forgiven *must* admit his or her wrongness or badness.
>
> *Convention #2:* The person to be forgiven *must* express genuine remorse (or at least has to do a good job of sounding remorseful).
>
> *Convention #3:* The person to be forgiven *must* verbally apologize.
>
> *Convention #4:* The person to be forgiven may be required to repeat the apology many times for an uncapped period of time, perhaps an entire life time.

Convention #5: The person to be forgiven vows never to make the mistake again.

Convention #6: The person to be forgiven is required to do something to make up for or *atone* for the mistake. This might involve playing an inferior role, buying a present, performing special favors, having constant make-up sex, going to counseling or whatever else the forgiver wants to impose.

Unfortunately, there's no social obligation for the offended person to actually forgive the wrong doer, and this is why social forgiveness is such a raw deal. So if just one of these rules is left out, the forgiver is justified in denying or delaying forgiveness. Even when all the rules are met, there's still no guarantee the forgiver will comply. The forgiver can stay hurt and upset for as long as subjectively deemed appropriate. What's more, even though the offended person may eventually express the *I forgive you* words, he/she can still hold a grudge and can still continue to demand acts of atonement. This is fake forgiveness extraordinaire.

When mistakes are made, terms like *I'm sorry, I apologize,* or *I forgive you* are expected. If you don't use the conventional words, it can easily make things worse by escalating anger, fueling resentment and generating even more bad feelings. Don't expect other people to understand the difference between fake forgiveness and authentic forgiveness, and it's not your job to explain it or to correct them. Just don't confuse the social convention of saying forgiveness words with the act of forgiveness, because it isn't. The social forgiveness words have one and only one purpose, and it's not forgiveness. Rather, it's to either assign blame or to accept it. Blame is an attack, which is hate. No wonder forgiveness has such a bad name.

Consider the real life saga of celebrity pro golfer, Tiger Woods, who got in a heap of personal and professional trouble for being a hound dog bad boy. Woods had it all: perfect career, perfect wife, perfect family, perfect bank account, perfect fame and the perfect collection of hot women on the side. A wife from another generation might have turned a blind eye and put up with it, but former wife Elin Nordegren wanted something else. She wanted monogamy, not a pretense of monogamy. Woods wanted the attention and company of many women.

The underlying problem to be solved was that Nordegren and Woods wanted different things. Society judged Woods as bad and wrong for his desire, while Nordegren was judged as good and superior for hers. Of course, Nordegren had the convention of marriage to help her out. A breach of an exclusive love contract is the most grievous assault on the dream of special love we're all having. Even more, the 7th Commandment from the Christian and Jewish traditions explicitly prohibits adultery. This is widely interpreted and accepted as a rule *(or a condition on love)* given to us directly from God, which makes adultery the worst kind of sin, the kind that puts you in hell forever. God was on Nordegren's side. Every married woman was on Nordegren's side. Every talking head commentator was on Nordegren's side. Even Woods' mom was upset with him. The social pressure on Woods to accept blame was extreme. Not surprisingly, he quickly caved to it. These are excerpts from the public apology statement he made on TV:

> I am deeply sorry for my irresponsible and selfish behavior...my behavior has been a personal disappointment...I have let you down... I know I have severely disappointed all of you...for all that I have done, I am so sorry. I have a lot to atone for...
>
> Tiger Woods

Even though Woods played his part and accepted the blame for being bad and wrong, he did not get forgiven and he did not receive an outpouring of love. More accurately, he didn't receive any love. The public didn't stop judging him. His wife left him anyway and took half his money. His girlfriends turned against him. His business endorsements and contracts dried up. If anything, Woods' downfall made people glad. *He deserved it. He had it coming.* Woods thinks he's bad, too. You can see it in his golf performance, which deteriorated immediately after the upsetting event.

We already know that Love is harmless and that God puts no conditions on his Love, even the condition of not committing adultery. It's not God's Will for Tiger Woods to suffer for his mistakes or for us to condemn him. Woods does the thankless service of disillusioning us. He gives us the privilege of seeing him *as he is* rather than how we fantasize him to be. It's a gift because we now have the pleasure of *going with God*, accepting Woods, and extending our love to him anyway. This is where the rubber hits the road. It's how you come to know and experience yourself as a loving being, and it only happens under fire. You need the pressure and the challenge of disillusionment to choose to be love anyway. How else will you recognize yourself as a loving being?

Today you will have the opportunity to forgive someone who disillusioned you. Forgiveness happens in your mind, so no verbal or written communication with the person is required. More than anything else, the forgiveness of another is the experience of self as Love because you are the one who's providing the Love that's missing. It's always and only about you.

DAY 17 STOPPING PRACTICE

MIND: The skill of the mind is to make a decision and hold it.

1. If needed, refresh your stopping intention. Then write it out three times. At the end of your statement, add the phrase *God is the strength in which I heal. I give my intention to my Christ-self to fulfill for me.*

2. Say your intention out loud three times. Again, do it with a little style.

3. Play one of your visualization rejection exercises in your mind.

4. Decide what kind of day you want it to be. Then ask your Christ-self to give it to you.

SPIRIT: The skill of the spirit is to experience an instant of inner peace so that you can turn off the ego and connect with your Christ self.

Your goal for today is a total of 15 minutes of meditation. Do one 8-minute period early in the day and another 7-minute meditation period later on, whenever it's convenient. In addition, recite your meditation phrase 12 times throughout the day, which is approximately once every hour. Do your communion exercise after a meditation period when your mind is peaceful and relaxed.

Today's meditation phrase

Forgiveness is the key to happiness.

Communion question

Teacher, what does my Father Will me to know about forgiveness of another?

Remember to capture your response in your *Miracle Stopping Journal.*

HEART: The skill of the heart is to make self happy. Your happiness is the most important thing in the world and cannot be sacrificed for any reason.

Happiness is blocked by the guilt you hold in your mind for yourself and by the anger you hold in your mind towards another. We begin the process of eliminating these blocks by examining the anger you hold in your mind for another and by offering forgiveness to this person. Forgiveness is accomplished by undoing your judgmental thought, which is another way of saying you change your mind. The following steps are provided solely for your convenience. The steps are helpers, but they're not mandatory. No forgiveness ritual is implied or intended.

1. Pick any person, living or dead, who angers you in some way.

   Briefly summarize what this person did to disappoint, disillusion or anger you. Did this person break a *rule* of specialness in some way?

2. List every single disturbance concerning this person, whether it's petty or grand. Don't leave anything out.

3. When your list is done, go back and read each disturbance, slowly, one at a time. Briefly shine light from you mind on each disturbance as you read it.

4. Think of at least one thing that you like or respect about this person. Write it down.

5. Write a statement of gratitude to this person for bringing you to forgiveness.

6. Insert the person's first name twice into the following phrase. When you're ready, slowly and calmly say the phrase.

In the holiness of God's light, I forgive _____ and I bless _____.

BODY: The skill of the body is to use physical tension to diffuse physical tension.

Today's exercise: Aerobic

Activity: Brisk walking with five 1-minute intervals of light jogging.

See below for minute-by-minute walk/jog guidelines

Time: 20 minutes

Minutes 1-4	Brisk Walking
Minute 5	Light Jogging
Minute 6-7	Brisk Walking
Minute 8	Light Jogging
Minute 9-10	Brisk Walking
Minute 11	Light Jogging
Minute 12-13	Brisk Walking
Minute 14	Light Jogging
Minute 15-16	Brisk Walking
Minute 17	Light Jogging
Minute 18-20	Brisk Walking

Pedometer people: Add anothr 250 steps today. This is a total of + 2,000 from your starting point. At the end of the day, record your actual step performance in your *Miracle Stopping Journal.*

As always, write about your exercise experience. Notice and comment on the increase in intensity.

Day 18

MORE POWER SKILL OF THE HEART

Connection makes you happy and
spiritual forgiveness restores connection

To forgive is to overlook. Look, then, beyond the error and do not let your
perception rest on it, for you will believe what your perception holds.

A COURSE IN MIRACLES

Excuse the rude topic, but have you ever been constipated? Last fall I took a two-day fall foliage trip up the Maine coast with my husband and another couple. Along the way, I found out my girlfriend travel buddy hadn't pooped for several days. She was suffering, constantly, from that unpleasant, plugged up feeling. We were on a driving trip that required long periods of sitting, so it wasn't the most accommodating situation. Even though she kept trying to go to the bathroom, it always involved pain and strain and never quite worked. In addition to being physically uncomfortable, my friend was also mildly alarmed by the prospect of being at increased risk of colon cancer. After I got home and flipped through my digital pictures of our vacay, I noticed that my friend wasn't smiling in any of them. When you can't poop, you're miserable.

Elimination is an essential life function. Essential means that waste removal is mandatory, not optional. Waste *must be* processed out of your body; otherwise it turns into a toxic poison that makes you uncomfortable and sick. It can even kill you. Think about all those people on dialysis who have to use a machine to process their waste. A high performing elimination system that gets waste out of your body is a physical priority. And a high performing forgiveness system that gets the hateful waste out of your mind is a mental and spiritual priority.

In addition to being toxic, the inability to process waste of any kind is also monumentally distracting. Think of how seeing lots of litter on the road distorts your experience. When you're upset, the emotional litter in your mind likewise distorts the quality of your life experience. Sometimes I have the unreal image of poop magically traveling up to my brain cells and clogging them up. Of course, this doesn't happen, but it *seems like* it happens because my thinking gets so plugged up and uncomfortable. The one and only relief for physical waste is to get it out of your body, just like the one and only relief for mental waste is to get it out of your mind. You can't hang on to mental waste and pretend everything is okay, because it's not. Spiritual forgiveness gets the mental waste out of your mind.

Mark Twain said that elimination is the most under-rated satisfaction. Everyone knows this, but we never talk about it. Even newborn babies intuitively feel better after they poop. In fact, getting rid of any kind of waste feels good, whether it's the kind of waste that's in our yards, on our roads, or in the mind. Mental and emotional waste comes from life situations we perceive as unfair or unjust, and is more commonly referred to as a grudge. The purpose of spiritual forgiveness is to eliminate mental and emotional wasting. Your part is to clean up the pollution in your own dirty mind and to keep our world free of your garbage. Former U.S. president Harry Truman is famous for saying *the buck stops here*. Spiritual forgiveness is the opportunity to make the buck stop with you. If you don't end the hate in your mind, who will? It must end with you.

Unlike social forgiveness, spiritual forgiveness has nothing to do with the determination of rightness or wrongness, and it doesn't involve correction of another, either. The only correction is in your own mind because you're changing your hateful thought to a benign and loving one. This is done by *overlooking the blame for a problem and getting right down to the practical business of solving the problem.* Overlooking blame is not rocket science, which is a good thing because that means everyone can do it. That said, overlooking of blame is a difficult spiritual concept to understand because it gets confused, erroneously, with overlooking problems and letting them go unsolved. The difference is that you're not passively letting your problems go unresolved. Rather, you're letting go of the blame and annoyance for having to deal with the problem.

If you come to one of my *Get Extreme Stopping Results* boot camps, and I hope you do, you'll see my three ceramic monkeys on display. I use them to demonstrate what it means to overlook. One monkey has his hands over his eyes. The second monkey has his hands over his mouth. The third monkey has his hands over his ears. The classic representation of *see no evil, speak no evil, hear no evil* is a demonstration of overlooking. The monkeys overlook evil by refusing to see it, refusing to hear it, refusing to talk about it. Evil doesn't get any attention or energy from the monkeys, and this makes it less important and less real. Most people don't immediately *get* how to see evil and overlook it, but for now, take it on faith that it's possible to organize your life, solve your problems, and get what you want while at the same time overlooking the urge to blame others for your difficulties.

Here's an example of how overlooking of blame works in real life. Let's say that one night while you were out having dinner at a friend's house your teenage son and one of his friends went rogue and lit a campfire in your backyard to make s'mores. By accident, a spark from the campfire flew onto the roof of your garage, and started a fire. By the time you got home, the fire department had already arrived and put out the fire, but your garage was ruined. There was also water and smoke damage to your house. Luckily, no one got hurt.

Your automatic ego response is to blame your son and to hold a grudge against him. After all, many mistakes were made. He lit a fire without your knowledge or permission. He didn't have adequate safety precautions in place, and he created a lot of extra, unnecessary work and expense for you. You feel justified getting mad at your son for creating such a disaster. It's possible, however, to solve your fire problem and to respond to your son without making a judgment of his badness or wrongness and without getting angry. You can salvage what's left in your garage without hate in your mind. You can talk to your teenager and find out how the accident happened without hate in your mind. You can put preventive measures in place so it doesn't happen again, all without hate. Your son can be counseled, educated, and disciplined all without hate. New family rules can be developed and implemented without hate. Your insurance claim can be processed without hate. A loan for extra money can be processed without hate. Your garage can be repaired without hate. These are all active, non-passive steps you can take to solve the problem at hand. What's different is that you're not making your teenager bad or wrong while you're at it. See how overlooking works? It's so subtle, you could easily miss it.

Hate adds no value to the solution. It does nothing to accelerate the problem-solving process or to make it easier. It does nothing to restore your joyful happy heart. Instead, it gives you something you don't want. You instantly get back the grudge energy you put out. When you extend a hateful grudge, what do you expect to come back to you? Do you expect kindness and good things to come to you from this person that you hate? No, you expect the worst. The ego's system of justice is *an eye for an eye*, and people always expect a grudge for a grudge. Now multiply that expectation by everyone you grudge, which could be quite a long list, and you can more easily envision the wave of unhappy energy you're inviting into your world. It's the law of attraction on steroids. When you put out blaming, judgmental grudge thoughts, you get back blaming, judgmental grudge thoughts. Every little grudge brings still more turmoil, still more churning and still more bad feelings. It's a monumental disruption of peace that increases your fear, anxiety and separation, and it all gets in the way of stopping yourself.

Overlooking the mistakes and idiocy of others makes it possible to overlook your own mistakes and your own idiocy, and this is what makes it possible to correctly perceive yourself as a worthy, loving, innocent being. Yesterday we started with forgiveness of another because forgiving another softens your heart, and makes it easier to forgive yourself. What you give to another, you receive for yourself. Today you extend forgiveness to yourself. The love and gratitude you gave to another is the same love and gratitude you now give to yourself. So what if you made a mistake? Or several. Give the consequences of your mistake(s) to your Christ-self. He knows what to do with them. You don't. There's nothing to fear or to feel bad about. All things work for good when you give your judgments to Christ.

Be like the three monkeys and practice spiritual vision on yourself. Refuse to see your mistake. Refuse to hear it. Refuse to talk about it. Refuse to dwell on it. Your only responsibility is to undo the hate you have in your mind that you hold for yourself. Trust your own goodness and forgive yourself.

DAY 18 STOPPING PRACTICE

MIND: The skill of the mind is to make a decision and hold it.

1. Refresh you intention statement if you need to. Then write it out three times. At the end of your statement, add the phrase *God is the strength in which I live. I give my intention to my Christ-self to fulfill for me.*

2. Say your intention out loud three times. Scream it. Whisper it. Say it normally.

3. Play one of your visualization rejection exercises in your mind.

4. Decide what kind of day you want it to be, and ask your Christ-self to give it to you.

SPIRIT: The skill of the spirit is to experience an instant of inner peace so that you can turn off the ego and connect with your Christ self.

Your goal for today is a total of 16 minutes of meditation. You can do one long session or two 8-minute sessions, but do your best to complete the full 16-minute requirement. Repeat the meditation phrase 25 times, which is approximately once every half hour. Complete your communion exercise right after a meditation period when your mind is peaceful and relaxed.

Today's meditation phrase

My holy vision sees all things as pure, including myself.

Communion question

Teacher, what does my Father Will me to know about my guiltlessness?

Remember to capture your response in your *Miracle Stopping Journal.*

HEART: The skill of the heart is to make self happy. Your happiness is the most important thing in the world and cannot be sacrificed for any reason.

Today we eliminate the second block to happiness, which is the guilt you hold in your mind for yourself. Again, these self-forgiveness helping steps are provided for your convenience. None are essential and <u>no forgiveness ritual is intended</u>.

1. Pick an incident in your life that makes you feel guilty. Briefly summarize what you did to disappoint yourself.

2. List every single judgmental thought you hold against yourself, whether it's petty or grand. Don't leave anything out.

3. When your list is done, go back and read each disturbance, slowly, one at a time. Briefly shine light from your mind on each disturbance as you read it.

4. See yourself giving your list to the Christ. See Him smiling and shining love on you and your list. See Him showing you your mistakes don't matter.

5. Write down at least one thing that you like and respect about yourself.

6. Write a statement of gratitude to yourself for your willingness to forgive.

7. When you're ready, slowly and calmly say this phrase:

In the holiness of God's light,
I fully forgive myself.
I fully bless myself.
I am worthy of every goodness.

BODY: The skill of the body is to use physical tension to diffuse physical tension.

Go to www.powertostop.com/tools if you need instruction.

Type exercise:	Strength Conditioning
Activity:	Calisthenics at home, a DVD workout, or weight training on a machine circuit at a health club
Time:	20 minutes minimum

Warm-up

• 5 minutes of abdominal work

• 10 minutes of lower body work

• 5 minutes of arm work

Pedometer people: You know the drill. Add another 250 steps today. This is a total of + 2,250 from your starting point. At the end of the day, record your actual step performance in your *Miracle Stopping Journal.*

As always, write about your exercise experience.

Day 19

THE POWER SKILL OF THE BODY

Freedom from absorption with the body

...the body is a learning device for the mind. Learning devices are not l
essons in themselves. Their purpose is merely to facilitate learning.
A COURSE IN MIRACLES

My mom was seriously sick for about a year before she died. I call it her fading
period. She could hardly walk, and she didn't even have the energy to do her
favorite sitting activities like reading, crocheting or playing cards. Getting in and
out of bed was a struggle for her and so was just getting through the day. Her daily
life contracted around monitoring her aches and pains and attention to the dismal
condition of her body. What could she eat that didn't make her sick? What position
could she take that didn't aggravate her pain? How would she get to the bathroom?
When could she take her next pill? My Mom suffered greatly from preoccupation
with her body. Bodily preoccupation is suffering for everyone. It's where we all get
lost and stuck.

The more attention and consciousness you put on your body, the more you suffer. The less attention and consciousness you put on your body, the less you suffer. Bottom line: suffering is ended by taking your attention off your body. It's not possible to be completely free of attention to the body, but a *just do it and forget it* attitude makes it possible to be mostly free of it. Each day a small amount of time is devoted to taking care of your physical self through physical activity. This self-care is similar to brushing your teeth, washing your hair and other physically-oriented tasks. You do it, and then you're done with it. After you brush your teeth, you don't think about your teeth anymore. After you take care of your body, you don't have to think about it anymore either. A miniscule amount of self-care frees you from absorption and obsession with your body and its endless sensations.

It's worth remembering that transcendence of ego happens in your mind, not in your body. Communion with your Christ-self happens in your mind, not your body. Stopping yourself happens in your mind, not your body. If you're absorbed with the body and its sensations, your attention is in the wrong place. The trip to heaven is made without the body, and your body is not what's important about you. Still, your body is part of your Earthly experience, and there are many documented and highly motivational reasons to take care of it. Most of them don't have much to do with stopping your out-of-control behavior, but they nonetheless have the power to move you to action and consequently have value. People take care of the body to lose weight; to look better; to attract mates; to achieve better sports or sex performance; to get stronger; to be more flexible; to have more endurance; to be less vulnerable to disease and injuries; to slow down the aging process, and/or to honor the structure where the Christ-self dwells. Much has already been said and written about physical objectives like these. They're not specifically addressed here because the primary reason for working *with* your body is to minimize or eliminate impulsive, self-destructive tension.

The lesson you learn *through* your body is how to *accept* and *deal* with this tension in a more creative way. Okay, maybe you also want to look a little better, too, and this will definitely happen for you. But mostly you want to train your body to generate more energy and to process energy more efficiently so you don't experience so many impulsive misfires. The paradox of daily physical activity is that it both invigorates and relaxes the body. Invigoration is the feeling of aliveness. When you accept and channel aliveness through regular physical activity, it's saying a big giant yes to life. Aliveness is always experienced as a lift. It literally and figuratively makes you more buoyant. You don't need happy pills to get you up out of the muck. You need a happy body, one that's filled to the brim with life energy. There's a direct relationship between your capacity to take in life, generate more energy, and your feelings of well-being.

Daily physical activity also relaxes the body. It does this by temporarily creating tension and then releasing it. Sustained physical activity puts a demand for extra work on the body. This is manufactured tension. As soon as the activity stops, the manufactured tension is released. The bonus is that any residual stress and tension stored in your body gets released, too. It's called the relaxation response. When you relax yourself in this way, a lot of your impulsivity gets flushed away along with the release of manufactured tension. Does it all go away? Maybe not, but there's definitely less, and less is better because it's easier for you to manage.

And lastly, daily physical activity changes the crazy mixed up emotional messages you receive because it changes your chemical messaging system. Hormones are the chemical messengers that regulate your mood and the way your body processes energy. Exercise releases *feel good* brain chemicals like endorphins, adrenaline, serotonin and dopamine, which elevate your mood. One study proved that 30 minutes of intense exercise is just as effective at improving mood as medication. And another study recently done by the University of Vermont showed a more lasting effect of exercise on mood. Two groups were studied. Each had 24 students. One group did 20 minutes of moderate intensity exercise on a bike, and the other group did nothing. The mood of both groups was measured immediately after the exercise group finished and then at 1, 2, 4, 8, 12 and 24-hour intervals. The exercise group had the biggest improvement in mood right after the exercise session, and although it lessened, the exercisers were able to sustain the improvement in mood for 12 hours. That's really an amazing discovery! Researchers say it's *an especially important finding for people who have depression.* And it's an especially important finding for you, too. If you're feeling bad about something, go exercise.

It's a no-brainer. Daily physical activity *must* become a part of your life. Six days a week. Every week. No exceptions. I've been coaching you to avoid the trap of establishing new routines and rituals for yourself, but ignore this advice when it comes to exercise. You're more likely to engage in physical activity if you get into a fixed, predictable routine. For one thing, on-the-fly planning of physical activity is a lot of unnecessary work, and for another, it creates too many opportunities for not doing it. Avoid the torment of making daily when/where decisions by making one decision now. Figure out when and where activity best fits in your life today, and get it over with. Schedule it into your calendar. Then, all that's left is to *just do it.*

Your prescription for daily physical activity involves the three variables of time, mode and intensity. Time is how long you're going to do it. Mode is what you're going to do. Intensity is how hard you're going to work. It's best, but not always possible, to make a sustained time commitment. Sustained means there are no breaks in between when you start and when you finish your physical activity. For most people, it's easier to do a physical activity session all at once. Also, you'll get a better relaxation result if you concentrate your activity in one session. A minimum of 10-minutes and a maximum of 60-minutes are recommended. 10-minutes will barely do the trick, but if it's all you want to do, then so be it. Anything over 60 minutes puts you at risk of burn-out. 30-minutes is ideal, and *The Power to Stop* program progressively gets you closer and closer to the 30-minute target.

There are three basic modes or types of physical activity: aerobic, strength training and flexibility. All are equally important. Aerobic exercise creates tension in your cardiovascular system by asking you to temporarily pump more blood. Depending on how hard you work, you can increase your flow by anywhere from 20% to 80%. This pumping action is big, vital energy. Strength training creates tension by putting an extra, temporary demand on your skeletal muscles. Whenever your muscles get tired or *fatigued*, your muscles do the work of adapting to the extra load by getting stronger and leaner. This growth action is big, vital energy. Flexibility creates tension by putting extra, temporary stress on your joints to expand them slightly beyond the normal range of motion. This expansion action is big, vital energy. An ideal physical activity program features all three modes because together they give you the most comprehensive energizing and deep relaxation effect.

The program you've been following in *The Power to Stop* features three days of aerobic activity, two days of strength training, one day of flexibility, and a day off. The three-day emphasis on aerobic activity is because walking is free and just about everyone can do it. The program could just as easily and effectively be changed to two days of aerobic activity, three days of strength training and one day of flexibility or one where flexibility predominates. When *The Power to Stop* is finished, you can change your weekly plan to whatever works for you or to whatever mode(s) you most prefer. Ideal is best, but if all you like is yoga, then do yoga. If riding a bike makes your heart sing, then ride a bike. If you like yoga and biking, do them both. It's more important to do <u>something</u> and to feel good about what you're doing than to angst about whether your physical activity program is perfect.

This brings us to the last physical activity description, which is intensity or how hard you work. The goal with intensity is to work hard enough to get a relaxation result, but not so hard that you hurt yourself or that you burn yourself out. Think of intensity as a minimum and maximum *range* of hardness. Use an imaginary scale of one to ten to estimate how hard you're working. One is no exertion and ten is the maximum you're capable of. Target an intensity range of six-seven-eight, with six being the least you ask of yourself and eight being the most you safely ask of yourself. You should feel like you're making a decent effort, but not a killer effort. There are other, more standardized ways to measure intensity, too. Aerobic activity is measured by *percentage of maximum heart rate*. Strength training is measured by how much work you can do before you reach *muscle failure*, the point where your muscles won't perform. And flexibility is measured by your maximum *range of motion*, which is how much you can move your joints before you experience strain. If you're unfamiliar with these terms and how to implement them, you can read an exercise book, but the best way to learn more is by doing: join a health club, take some classes, watch a DVD or hire a personal trainer.

In all cases and no matter how it's measured, intensity produces the desired relaxation response through an increase in work or pressure. The harder you work, the more tension you create, the more tension you release. This is the one place where more effort is appropriate and better. Brief periods of high intensity movements enable you to achieve greater systemic relaxation, but working harder is – well, it's hard, and it also puts you at risk for more injuries. For now, gently ease into asking yourself to work a little harder. Some people come to enjoy it, and some people don't. Figure out what camp you're in and keep going. From this day forward, regular physical activity is going to be a part of your life. Accept it. Embrace it. Make the best of it. It's another tangible demonstration of the love you shower on yourself.

> Say it to yourself now and never forget it:
> I can do anything I want with my body.
> Arnold Schwarzenegger

DAY 19 STOPPING PRACTICE

MIND: The skill of the mind is to make a decision and hold it.

1. Write your stopping intention three times. At the end of your statement, add the phrase *God is the strength in which <u>I love myself</u>. I give my intention to my Christ-self to fulfill for me.*

2. Say your intention out loud three times. You know what to do. Make it fun and interesting for yourself.

3. Play one of your visualization rejection exercises in your mind, but do it with attitude. Make it funky or rude or silly.

4. Decide the kind of day you want to have, and ask your Christ-self to give it to you.

SPIRIT: The skill of the spirit is to experience an instant of inner peace so that you can turn off the ego and connect with your Christ self.

Your goal for today is a total of 18 minutes of meditation. You can do one long session, two 9-minute sessions, or three 6-minute sessions. Decide for yourself how to implement your meditation goal. Repeat the meditation phrase 24 times, which is approximately once every half-hour. Complete your communion exercise right after your first meditation period when your mind is peaceful and relaxed.

Today's meditation phrase

I am not a body, I am free, for I am still as God created me.

Communion question

Teacher, what does my Father Will me to know about my body?

Remember to capture your response in your *Miracle Stopping Journal.*

HEART: The skill of the heart is to make self happy. Your happiness is the most important thing in the world and cannot be sacrificed for any reason.

I just read an article that claims gratitude increases your happiness by 25%. Don't believe this for a minute because gratitude increases your happiness by a full 100%! A grateful thought is a loving thought, and love always makes you happy. Set your timer for 2 minutes. Write about everyone and everything in your life, present or past, that you're grateful for.

BODY: The skill of the body is to use physical tension to diffuse physical tension.

Today's exercise:	Aerobic
Activity:	Brisk walking with five 1-minute intervals of light jogging
	See below for minute-by-minute walk/jog guidelines
Time:	20 minutes

Minutes 1-4	Brisk Walking
Minute 5	Light Jogging

Minute 6-7	Brisk Walking
Minute 8	Light Jogging
Minute 9-10	Brisk Walking
Minute 11	Light Jogging
Minute 12-13	Brisk Walking
Minute 14	Light Jogging
Minute 15-16	Brisk Walking
Minute 17	Light Jogging
Minute 18-20	Brisk Walking

Pedometer people: Today's goal is with another 250 steps, which is a total of + 2,500 from your starting point. At the end of the day, record your actual step performance in your *Miracle Stopping Journal.* As always, write about your exercise experience.

Day 20
MAKE EACH DAY COUNT
Live your daily power code

Your day is not at random. It is set by what you choose to live it with.
A COURSE IN MIRACLES

About 15 years ago I lived next door to a Hungarian immigrant named Tibor, an unusually active and disciplined 75-ish man. I know this about Tibor because I watched him, secretly, almost every day. I wish I could tell you my spying was part of a grand adventure. Regrettably, it had more to do with the convenient position of my desk, which was right under a big Palladian window in my home office. All I ever had to do was look up from my computer to see a view of the woods across the street, and this is how I began my private study of Tibor's religious comings and goings.

Every morning I would see Tibor and his big German shepherd walk into the woods; then 20 minutes later I would see them come out. Tibor always started his walking trek empty handed, and he always ended it carrying a couple of old logs or large branches that he found lying around. Once in a while he would haul in a chain saw so that he could cut big trees that fell on the ground into portable chunks. Tibor carried all the wood to his home, and then he carefully stacked under his porch so he could use it in his fireplace. I don't recall Tibor ever actually purchasing a cord of wood. His modest daily wood-collecting task amply met his need for firewood. Tibor is memorable because he never took a day off. Not ever. Summer or winter, it made no difference, and we're talking about the northeast, where winter is frigid and harsh. Rain didn't stop him. Snow either. The dog got walked every day, and the wood got collected every day, no matter what. I could see from Tibor's relaxed gait and demeanor that these two tasks weren't a monumental effort or burden. Walking the dog and collecting wood was Tibor's job, and he did it with ease.

Your job is to live your daily power code. Like Tibor, you can accomplish a lot by doing a little every day. When you make a small but consistent daily effort, your job gets done, and it gets done easily. Every day you take the same four simple stopping steps. Over and over, whether you feel like it or not, you do the steps. Whether the conditions in your life are conducive or not, you do them. Whether you see a result right away or not, you do them.

When you fill your days with deliberate, purposeful actions, your life counts. It satisfies, too. Say goodbye to mindless robotic gestures, and say hello to living in a meaningful way. Your goal for making your life count is always the same: to live your daily power code to the best of your ability. *Daily* means it's something you do every day. *Power* means that you're consciously producing an intended result And *Code* is the agreement you make with yourself about how you're going to live. You live your daily power code before you stop yourself. You live your daily power code when you stop yourself. You live your daily power code after you stop yourself. You live your daily power code if you make a mistake. The goal of stopping guides you, but in a sense it doesn't matter, because you'll always be living the same way no matter where you are on the stopping continuum.

You've been living and practicing your daily power code from Day 1 of *The Power to Stop* program. Today you'll pull it all together and personalize the code so that by the end of the 30-day program, you know exactly how to progress. Make your personalization decisions in terms of *the least you'll do for yourself* on any one day, not the most that you ask of yourself. There will be many days when you'll be highly inspired to do more than the least, and that's fine. The least that you do for yourself is your baseline.

THE SKILL OF THE MIND

You've been exposed to three tools for making a decision and holding it. This includes

♥ Formulating a stopping intention statement and expressing it with your voice, in writing and in your mind.

♥ A visualization exercise where you reject or not do the behavior you want to stop.

♥ Deciding up-front what you want from your day and asking for it.

Decide now

1. Determine the least amount of time you'll devote to keeping yourself on track every day. Express your commitment in minutes.

2. Determine the tools you will use.

THE SKILL OF THE SPIRIT

You've been exposed to three tools to experience a peaceful state of mind and for strengthening your connection to your Christ-self. This includes

♥ Meditating with directive and uplifting thought statements.

♥ Using the Holy Instant of peace to stop your automatic response to impulsive tension.

♥ Communing with your Christ-self for direction and wisdom.

Decide now

1. To use the Holy Instant of peace whenever you need it.

2. To commune with your Christ-self frequently, and especially when you have a problem to solve or whenever you need to make a major decision.

3. Determine the least amount of time you'll devote to daily meditation.

THE SKILL OF THE HEART

You've been exposed to multiple tools for the experience of happiness

- ♥ Awareness that love is harmless

- ♥ Envisioning a positive outcome

- ♥ A focus on happy memories

- ♥ Gratitude

- ♥ Asking for what you want instead of complaining about what you don't want

- ♥ Saying no to others

- ♥ Awareness of personal passion

- ♥ Engaging in life activities that make you happy and that relate to your passion

- ♥ Perceiving disappointments as a wake-up call

- ♥ Forgiveness of another

- ♥ Forgiveness of self

- ♥ Peaceful relationships

Decide now

1. To take responsibility for your own happiness
2. To engage in at least one happiness activity every day of your life

THE SKILL OF THE BODY

You've been exposed to three modes of physical activity for releasing physical tension and for minimizing absorption with the body.

- ♥ Aerobic mode, including an increase in daily steps

- ♥ Strength training mode

- ♥ Flexibility mode

Decide now

1. Determine the least amount of time you'll devote to daily physical activity. Express your commitment in minutes.

2. Determine the mode(s) you will use and a weekly activity plan.

Go to www.powertostop.com/tools and print out a copy of the *Daily Power Code Tracking Form*. Record your decisions in the appropriate columns. Then use the form to track your actual performance against your plan.

When you live your daily power code, your actions speak for you. Tibor didn't speak about his daily wood collecting activities. He demonstrated it. When people observe you making the same consistent choices, day after day, you speak loudly. Like Tibor, you do it without words. There's great power in silently walking the talk. All the support you ever wanted is available to you when your will becomes tangible and discernible to others. Attention comes to you, automatically, without asking for it. Glory comes to you, automatically. Respect is offered, automatically. All this comes to you through your own personal stopping demonstration, which is made possible by living your daily power code.

DAY 20 STOPPING PRACTICE

MIND: The skill of the mind is to make a decision and hold it.

1. If necessary, refresh your stopping intention and write it three times. At the end of your statement, add the phrase *God is the strength in which I see the light. I give my intention to my Christ-self to fulfill for me.*

2. Say your intention out loud three times. Sing it like you're in an opera.

3. Play one of your visualization rejection exercises in your mind. Again, with attitude. Make it funky, or rude or silly.

4. Decide what kind of day you want to have, and ask your Christ-self to give it to you.

SPIRIT: The skill of the spirit is to experience an instant of inner peace so that you can turn off the ego and connect with your Christ self.

Your goal for today is another 15 consistent minutes of meditation. Repeat the meditation phrase 12 times, which is approximately one per hour. Complete your communion exercise after a meditation period when your mind is peaceful and relaxed.

Today's meditation phrase

Light and joy and peace abide in me.

Communion question

Teacher, what does my Father Will me to know about gratitude?

Remember to capture your response in your *Miracle Stopping Journal.*

HEART: The skill of the heart is to make self happy. Your happiness is the most important thing in the world and cannot be sacrificed for any reason.

Gratitude makes you happy. Think of someone important in your life, either living or dead, and write a letter of gratitude to this person. Tell the person how he/she made your life better. Tell the person what you learned from him/her. Express your thanks. You have the option of privately keeping your letter in your *Miracle Stopping Journal* or if you feel comfortable and if the recipient is alive, you can send it to him/her.

BODY: The skill of the body is to use physical tension to diffuse physical tension.

Type exercise:	Flexibility
Activity:	Stretching or yoga poses
Time:	15 minutes minimum

Pedometer people: Today's goal is an additional 250 steps which is +2,750 steps over your starting point. At the end of the day, record your actual step performance in your *Miracle Stopping Journal*.

As always, write about your exercise experience.

Day 21

REVIEW OF WEEK THREE

...the goal is life, which has no end.

A COURSE IN MIRACLES

As you know, reviews are designed to reinforce and consolidate the ideas presented in the previous week.

Week three accomplishments

♥ You progressively increased your practice of the four stopping skills.

♥ You gave your stopping intention to your Christ-self for fulfillment.

♥ You forgave another, which is love.

♥ You forgave yourself, which is love.

♥ You extended gratitude, which is love.

♥ You formulated your personal daily mind-spirit-heart-body power code plan and wrote it down.

Which weekly activity was most helpful to you?

DAY 21 STOPPING PRACTICE

MIND: The skill of the mind is to make a decision and hold it.

1. Today you'll craft your very own personal stopping prayer. It will replace your daily intention statement that you've been successfully using up until now. Successful praying isn't a matter of divine intervention or luck. It's another disciplined process for activating the same thought, over and over, about what you want. Here are some guidelines to consider.

    •   Continue to focus on what you want, not on what you don't want.

    •   Enlist the help of God, the Holy Spirit, Angels, Jesus, Buddha or whatever name you most prefer.

    •   Again, use words that are meaningful and inspiring to you.

    •   Keep it short. No longer than 1 minute at the maximum.

    •   If you happen to have a natural affinity for rhyming, use it.

Three examples of stopping prayers are provided below. Use them, modify them, or write your own.

Prayer to Angels

Angels above me, angels below me, angels all around me.
Angels shower me with love and give me their stillness.
Stillness heals me and makes me whole. Amen

Prayer to Jesus

All power, peace, and purpose come to me whenever I need it.
I need it now, brother Jesus. I am healed by your exquisite stillness,
which fills me to the brim. Amen.

Prayer for inner peace

Today is the day I choose stillness.
Now is the moment I experience stillness.

Stillness flows in my blood and penetrates my DNA.
God's stillness is the healing solution I seek. Amen

2. Copy your stopping prayer a total of three times in your *Miracle Stopping Journal*. Then copy it one more time onto a piece of paper or index card so that you can take it out and read it whenever necessary.

3. Read your stopping prayer at least three times during the day: at lunch, at dinner and before you go to bed at night.

SPIRIT: The skill of the spirit is to experience an instant of inner peace so that you can turn off the ego and connect with your Christ self.

Read the six meditation phrases that were provided during your second week. Pick the one that's most meaningful for you, follow the time directions associated with the phrase, and use it for your meditation today.

Write this phrase in your *Miracle Stopping Journal* and explain why it's important to you.

HEART: The skill of the heart is to make self happy. Your happiness is the most important thing in the world and cannot be sacrificed for any reason.

As you now know, gratitude makes you happy. Yesterday you wrote a letter of gratitude to someone else; today you write a letter of gratitude to yourself. Be sweet. Be lavish. Be over the top. You can't be too thankful to yourself.

BODY: The skill of the body is to use physical tension to diffuse physical tension.

Physical rest day. No activity required.

Summarize your weekly exercise experience. Note the type of exercise you most prefer and where you see yourself headed with physical activity.

RATE YOUR 3ⁿᵈ WEEK

Use a scale of (1) low to (10) high. Rate your weekly experience on the program, and briefly explain why you gave this rating.

What are you doing well?

What can you do better?

Day 22

MISTAKES STRENGTHEN YOUR RESOLVE

Put your attention on the process, not the result

What can it be but arrogance to think your little errors cannot be undone.

A COURSE IN MIRACLES

B asset hounds are the world's cutest puppies. I love how they smell. I love the sweet little puppy noises they make. And mostly, I love how they cuddle in my lap and lavish me with dog kisses. It's a good thing basset puppies are so darn cute because this breed can be tough to housebreak. My Max dog stands out as the biggest, most badass housebreaking challenge of all. I did everything by the book with Max. He got taken out every hour. He got showered with affection and praise. He got food rewards for doing his business outside, on command. Despite this determined start, Max loved to lift his leg and pee on my furniture.

No matter what I did with Max, no matter how much I cleaned, no matter what products I used, Max stubbornly continued peeing on my furniture. This went on for months. It was infuriating. It was also wrecking my house, and I was getting pretty darn sick and tired of it. In my whole life, I never had such a difficult dog experience as the one I had with Max. Thoughts about hopelessness started creeping in. Maybe it was a mistake to get him. Maybe I should find Max a new place to live. Luckily for Max, I have my own stubborn streak, and I resolved to try one more thing before giving up on him. The answer to my prayers came in the form of an indoor invisible fence system. All I had to do was get Max a collar and position some portable boundary markers near the furniture. The situation with Max felt like a hopeless, unresolvable mistake, but it wasn't. A stopping solution existed, and I found it.

Your stopping mistakes might feel hopeless and unresolvable, too, but they aren't. A stopping solution exists, and you will find it. Albert Ellis, the famous psychologist, once said that *perfectionism is the root of all evil*. Coming face to face with your own imperfection is the most common and easy reason to give up or give in. But don't. Not now. Not ever. Nothing is accomplished by quitting. It doesn't solve your problem. It doesn't make you feel good about yourself. It doesn't make your life work better. All you get is delay and procrastination. In the end, you'll be right back here, at the same exact spot where your unresolved behavior problem keeps popping up. It's unavoidable. Resign yourself to dealing with it now.

If you take the smallest, most half-hearted step, you haven't given up on yourself. Keep taking small steps no matter what. Even though your demonstration of stopping may be less than ideal, you have not given up. This is why your half-hearted situation is hopeful and workable. Half a heart is better than no heart. Your willingness is there in your half heart. Notice your willingness. Be grateful for it. It's enough to re-launch yourself.

So what if you make a mistake? Mistakes are inevitable, especially when you're getting started, but they don't have to be treated like a big deal. Contain and minimize your mistakes by getting right back on track. Immediately! Don't linger or wallow in the error. Don't talk about it. Don't make up for it. Instead, *overlook it.* Just pick yourself up and keep going, without blinking an eye. When you treat your mistakes this way, no one notices. Not even you. The universal tendency is to endow your mistake (and everyone else's) with meaning and importance. Maybe you think it means you're weak or that you'll never learn stopping. This is all ego nonsense. A mistake is a waste of energy, that's all. Waste is waste. It's meaningless. Nothing. Resist the urge to make something out of nothing.

Remember the first time you ever rode a bike without training wheels? It took a few falls to find your balance, didn't it? The falls were nothing, right? It's highly unlikely you ever think about falling off your bike now or that you attach any significance to it. That's because bike-riding got easy-peasy once you learned how to hold your balance. Balance is the place where you hold yourself upright, without falling. It's learned by falling and then getting back up. Falling and getting back up. Every time you fall, you pick up another clue about where to position your body. In fact, *balance cannot be learned or found without falling.* Falls are an ordinary and natural part of the learning process. Remind yourself that you're still learning stopping. You learn by doing. Not by beating yourself up, and not by staying down and indulging your fall.

Consider these two, powerful corrective actions whenever you make a mistake. The first is to strengthen your intention by firmly making up your mind to stop yourself. Your biggest problem is your own indecision, and by that I mean you haven't fully made up your mind to stop yourself. Indecision is either being expressed as your inability to fully engage in the stopping process or as frequent time offs, which then throw you off balance. In either case, you want two opposing things. You want to indulge in the substance and you also want to stop yourself. This is conflict, and it weakens your power. In conflicted situations, the easiest choice predominates, and the easiest choice is not stopping. Make a firm decision to stop. Healing comes from your firm, whole decision.

The second corrective action is to put your attention on the 4-step daily stopping process and take it off the stopping result. Let the result come to you without any fussing and fretting. Instead of tormenting yourself, think about how completely you perform each of the four daily steps. How fully do you engage in them? How can you bring more energy and attention to your stopping practice? Every time you take a stopping step, you demonstrate your willingness to say yes to life, and you demonstrate your love of self. There is great value in this demonstration. Each time you take a stopping step you also accumulate a little more personal power. We already discussed how it's possible to store this energy. As your power builds, you eventually get a surge from your own energy reservoir. This surge enables you to *smash through* your resistance to a new level of performance. You'll get the feeling of *coming around*. Do the four steps, and expect the surge.

In the meantime, give your mistake to your Christ-self. He knows what to do with the consequences; you do not. Continue on your mission to pay more attention to your Christ-self and less attention to the sensations in your body. Find that quiet, peaceful place in your mind where your body ceases to demand your attention. The stronger your relationship and reliance on your Christ-self, the faster you release yourself from obsession with the body. Less obsession is definitely better. You already have all the preparation you need to make the connection to your Christ-self and to rely on it.

There is nothing your Christ-self cannot do. Keep going.

DAY 22 STOPPING PRACTICE

MIND: The skill of the mind is to make a decision and hold it

Say your stopping prayer, and then reinforce and turbo-charge your stopping intention with these four stopping boosts. This is a little more work than is typically asked of you, but if you're having stopping problems, remedial skill-building is just what you need.

Intention Boost #1: Journaling Exercise

Get out your *Miracle Stopping Journal* and brainstorm for one full page about how your life will be different when you stop yourself. This is what you want, and this is where you need to concentrate your thinking. Consider repeating this exercise every day until there is no doubt or conflict about what you want.

Intention Boost #2: Notice and reward what you're doing well

There's a reason Weight Watchers gives out stars to people who lose weight! Everyone likes to get noticed and appreciated for small accomplishments on a long path. You have to be your own audience and you have to give yourself your own gold stars. Which components of the *Power to Stop* program are you doing well? Are you exercising and meditating every day or at least most days? Are you more aware of going to the dark side to force the world to do your bidding? Are you fully engaged in doing something to make yourself happy every day? These are all quantum leaps. Notice and write down everything that's working. Draw a star for each activity you listed. Express gratitude to yourself for your effort and for the things you do well.

Intention Boost #3: Make stopping easier

How easy can you make stopping? Instead of asking yourself to stop for 30 days, ask yourself to stop for one full day. This is the easiest short-term goal. Once you stop for a day, you will know that stopping is doable, that it didn't kill you, and that it didn't make you unhappy. This kind of knowledge <u>must be</u> acquired through first-hand experience and cannot be given to you in a book. Each time you achieve a short stopping goal, it makes you stronger and more confident. Once you stop for a day, ask yourself to stop for two days. Once you get to two days, ask yourself to stop for a week. Once you get to a week, ask yourself to stop for two weeks or a month. Keep progressively increasing your short-term goal until you get to 30 consecutive days. Then you will have enough stopping experience under your belt to figure out how to proceed.

Intention Boost #4: Make a visualization of one successful day

What does one successful day look like? What does it feel like? How is a successful day different than what you're doing now? Make a quick visualization of the precise thing that you're doing differently on a successful day. Be sure to see yourself smiling at the end of it.

SPIRIT: The skill of the spirit is to experience an instant of inner peace so that you can turn off the ego and connect with your Christ-self.

Today's goal is a total of 20-minutes of meditation. Configure your meditation practice in any way that's convenient to you. It could be one long session, two 10-minute sessions, three 7-minute sessions, or any other variation.

Do your communion exercise after one of your meditation periods, when your mind is relaxed and still.

Today's meditation phrase

Your peace is with me, Father. I am safe.

Communion question

Teacher, what does my Father Will me to know about my mistakes?

HEART: The skill of the heart is to make self happy. Your happiness is the most important thing in the world and cannot be sacrificed for any reason.

Living in a relaxed, effortless way makes you happy. It's impossible to enjoy your daily life and to experience happiness from it when you race through your daily activities as fast as you're humanly able, just to quickly move on and get things done. Speed and rushing creates a subtle, but tangible tension and all forms of tension increase your tendency to be impulsive. Speeding also blocks your happiness because you never get to enjoy the present moment. One way to pre-empt this tension and to enjoy the moment is to give yourself more time to do things. You'll be doing this in one small way today. Pick any routine task that you normally perform in a rushed, robotic way and slow it down. It can be anything: loading the dishwasher, feeding your dog, putting on make-up, sex with your partner, eating, driving your car, or anything else you speed through.

Decide on your task, and then make these two simple intentions before you perform it.

1. For today only, treat your task as the most important activity in your life. How perfectly can you perform it? How long can you make it last? What can you do to make it enjoyable?

2. For today only, give yourself fully to the task. Giving yourself fully means that you invest everything you have in your performance. There's no resistance and no tuning out. Your full attention is on the task. Go into it with the intention of winning an Academy Award for exploiting the task to bring out what's best about you.

After you do the task, answer this series of questions about it:

What is the task? How did slowing down the speed work for you? Did you experience joy while performing the task in this way? If not, what could you have done to extract more enjoyment from your performance?

BODY: The skill of the body is to use physical tension to release physical tension.

This week you'll once again be slightly increasing the time and intensity of your exercise sessions. The combination of more time and greater effort will give you a bigger and more effective relaxation response, which is what you want. Here's a summary of your weekly activity schedule:

Day 22	*Day 23*	*Day 24*	*Day 25*	*Day 26*	*Day 27*	*Day 28*
Aerobic	*Strength*	*Aerobic*	*Strength*	*Aerobic*	*Flexibility*	*Day Off*

Mode:	Aerobic
Activity:	Brisk walking with five 2-minute intervals of light jogging
	See below for minute-by-minute walk/jog guidelines
Time:	25 minutes

Minutes 1-3	Brisk Walking

Minute 4-5	Light Jogging
Minute 6-7	Brisk Walking
Minute 8-9	Light Jogging
Minute 10-11	Brisk Walking
Minute 12-13	Light Jogging
Minute 14-15	Brisk Walking
Minute 16-17	Light Jogging
Minute 18-19	Brisk Walking
Minute 20-21	Light Jogging
Minute 22-25	Brisk Walking

Pedometer people: Add another 250 steps today. This is a total of + 3,000 steps from your starting point. At the end of the day, record your actual step performance in your *Miracle Stopping Journal.*

As always, write about your activity experience. Comment on your reaction to the increase in time and intensity.

Day 23

AN INVITATION TO TEACH

Your life as a shining example

To teach is to demonstrate...From your
demonstration others learn, and so do you.

A COURSE IN MIRACLES

This is the truth. We'll do more for others than we'll do for ourselves. There's nothing like company to get your house sparkling clean. There's nothing like a new love interest to get yourself looking good and pulled together. There's nothing like the reward of making big money to get yourself motivated to do an unpleasant job. We like the payoff, and we like the glory. It's an ego thing, and for a change, you can play to the ego and use this quirk to your advantage. Ego only performs *to get something*. It never does anything for nothing. Let your ego be turned on and inspired by the prospect of garnishing some top quality R-E-S-P-E-C-T and big time attention for yourself.

Stopping yourself for a sustained period of time automatically puts you on display. People notice. They assess. They want to know *how* you did it. They want to know *why* you did it. They want to know your special tricks and your personal pointers. Did you do it on your own or did you participate in a program? How many tries did it take? What kind of problems did you encounter? What did you do when you felt like giving up?

Be prepared to answer every kind of what, where, how, and when question. Even more, cultivate the awareness that you're playing an important, leadership role. Everyone teaches, but everyone isn't aware that teaching is going on. We think that teaching occurs in a classroom, by books and lectures, but this is only the transfer of facts and information. Teaching happens in only one way: by demonstration. Think about how you make decisions based on personal demonstration. Do you trust medical doctors who are overweight or who smoke? Do you trust financial experts who don't live well? Do you trust style experts who look like hell? Do you trust relationship experts who are divorced? Do you trust photographers who can't take a decent picture? The people we most trust are the ones who earn our trust by *walking the talk*. Experts who study problems but who haven't personally lived with them or successfully resolved them are less influential than people who *walk the talk*.

Your personal demonstration of stopping is your strongest calling card. Every time you act, you teach. Every time you resist an act, you teach. Your actions show others how to live or how not to live; what to seek and what to avoid. You're either inviting others to copy you or you are persuading them to find another way. Both are effective teaching modalities, but it makes you feel better about yourself when you teach the choice for aliveness and life rather than the choice for destruction and death. My parents, for example, both smoked. They were from the Great Depression era when smoking was cool and wasn't widely recognized as a health hazard. There was a constant haze of second-hand smoke in my girlhood home, and I vividly remember holding my breath whenever I had to walk through it. Every flat surface space had an ashtray that overflowed with ashes and half-smoked cigarette butts. For some reason, just looking at the piles of ashes was a tremendous turn-off for me. And cleaning them – oh my goodness -- it was unbearable. I never once bought a cigarette or tried smoking one because the whole smoking scene was so personally disgusting to me. My parents were my inspiration, and they inspired me with their actions, not their words. Even though their actions weren't about saving life, I got a life-saving message anyway. Can you see how teaching from demonstration cannot be avoided?

Like my parents, everyone has a built-in audience of students. Your audience includes your own family, friends, work associates, schoolmates, neighbors, service providers, and the community where you live. You teach your day-to-day audience. Your ongoing live demonstration of what works and what doesn't work is your invaluable service to others. The people in your personal sphere of influence save a vast amount of time that would otherwise be expended on trial and error just by watching you live wisely.

Begin to humbly think of yourself as a teacher and a role model for others. Without saying a word, you will teach. Without pushing or pulling, you will attract followers. Without presenting yourself as an expert, you will be treated like one. It happens through your everyday actions and through your quiet presentation of self. It's not arrogance, because you don't brag. It's not a burden, because you're not doing anything extra or out-of-the-ordinary. It's not demanding, because you don't expect anything of anybody. If people follow, fine. If not, fine. When you begin to think of yourself as a teacher or a role model, you begin to pay more attention to what you're doing. You may also work a little harder to get it right. Anything that serves to heighten your awareness and to strengthen your motivation is your advantage. Teachers spur themselves on and they spur other people on.

People desperately need to see a stopping example, and they need to see it from someone who's in their day-to-day range of experience. They can be inspired by you, a perfectly ordinary human being. You can be a teacher. If you live *The Power to Stop* program, you can teach it. That's all it takes. Nothing else is required – no special skills, no special talents. Who cares what celebrities accomplish through trainers, physicians, coaches, cooks and stylists? It's a huge advantage to have unlimited resources, but what about the average person who only has self to rely on? A cast of thousands at your beck and call is nice, but it's not necessary. You and your Christ-self are enough. By your example, you show that it's enough. This is a rare demonstration of living on purpose and with purpose. It's strength in action, and the world needs to see it. The world needs to see you! Who but you will show that bodily problems can be resolved through peace? You are the answer. You, my friend, you.

After you successfully complete *The Power to Stop* program, there are four teaching options available to you:

1. You can live as a quiet, informal model of stopping.

2. You can become a *Power to Stop* online coach. Coaches listen to others on the stopping path and provide useful feedback.

3. You can become a *Power to Stop* affiliate and sell the *Power to Stop* program to others. This is done primarily through your website or blog, and also by word-of-mouth. Affiliates make money simply by making others aware of *The Power to Stop* and by endorsing it.

4. You can buy a *Power to Stop* seminar license and teach the program in boot camps and seminars to others.

I would so enjoy and appreciate your fellowship on the stopping mountain. Go to www.powertostop.com/tools for more information about your teaching options.

DAY 23 STOPPING PRACTICE

MIND: The skill of the mind is to make a decision and hold it

1. Write your stopping prayer a total of three times in your *Miracle Stopping Journal*.

2. Read your stopping prayer at least three times during the day: at lunch, at dinner and before you go to bed.

3. Decide what kind of day you want it to be. Ask your Christ-self to give it to you.

SPIRIT: The skill of the spirit is to experience an instant of inner peace so that you can turn off the ego and connect with your Christ-self.

Today's goal is 20 minutes of meditation. Configure your meditation periods into two 10-minute intervals. Do your communion exercise after one of your meditation periods when your mind is relaxed and still.

Today's meditation phrase

I am the light of the world.

Communion question

Teacher, what does my Father Will me to know about shining my light for the world to see?

HEART: The skill of the heart is to make self happy. Your happiness is the most important thing in the world and cannot be sacrificed for any reason.

Write about an experience in your past where you copied someone or they copied you. What was copied? Why was it copied? How long did it take replicate the behavior? Did you recognize yourself as a teacher or as a student? Consider and write about how much easier it is to do something when you see someone else do it.

BODY: The skill of the body is to use physical tension to release physical tension.

Go to www.powertostop.com/tools if you need exercise direction.

Mode:	Strength training
Activity:	Calisthenics at home, DVD work out, or weight training on a machine circuit at a health club
Time:	25 minutes minimum
	• Warm-up
	• 5 minutes of abdominal work

- 10 minutes of lower body work

- 5 minutes of upper body work

- 5 minutes of arm work

Intensity: Try your best to get a maximum contraction from each of your strength training moves. This is a brief, 1 or 2 second pause, at the most intense moment in the exercise..

Pedometer people: Add another 250 steps today. This is a total of + 3,250 steps from your starting point.

As always, comment on your activity experience.

Day 24

LIVE WITH POWER, LOVE AND PURPOSE

Share your wisdom about the power skill of the spirit

The sign of Christmas is a star, a light in darkness. See it not outside yourself.
A COURSE IN MIRACLES

Every day for the past 24 days, you've been developing the skill of the spirit. You now know something about connecting to spirit that you can share with others.

♥ You know how to sit still in peace and how to use an uplifted thought to calm your mind.

♥ You know how to use the Holy Instant of peace to stop the automatic ego response to provocation.

♥ You know how to commune with your Christ-self for direction and wisdom.

♥ You know how to turn everything you don't want over to your Christ-self. He knows what to do with it. You don't.

It's time to teach what you know and thereby learn it more fully. Today you give the lesson. Your goal is to explain why the skill of the spirit enables you to stop yourself. Why should someone bother to learn about peace and use it? Start by sharing a real-life example of how peace and communion work for you, personally. Explain what you do. Explain why you do it. Explain what you get from it. Give simple direction others can follow.

Set your timer for two minutes and brainstorm what you know about the skill of the spirit in your *Miracle Stopping Journal*. Get your thoughts about spirit down on paper, and don't worry if you're saying them perfectly or not. When you're done brainstorming, polish and refine your writing so that others will enjoy reading it. And lastly, edit your message down to 1,000 words or less. When your message is as good as you can get it, go to www.stoppingnation.com. Register so that you can share your content with others. Then copy and post your message in the *Wisdom of the Spirit* category. Your lesson will be available for the general public to read.

DAY 24 STOPPING PRACTICE

MIND: The skill of the mind is to make a decision and hold it

1. Write your stopping prayer three times into your *Miracle Stopping Journal*.

2. If you haven't already memorized your stopping prayer, memorize it now.

3. Shut your eyes and slowly recite your stopping prayer out loud three times.

4. Offer your stopping prayer to your Christ-self for a blessing.

5. Silently recite your stopping prayer before lunch, before dinner and before you go to bed.

SPIRIT: The skill of the spirit is to experience an instant of inner peace so that you can turn off the ego and connect with your Christ-self.

Today's goal is 20-minutes of meditation. Configure your meditation time in any way that's convenient for you, as one session, multiple sessions, or as frequent repetitions of your thought statement. Do your communion exercise after one of your meditation periods, when your mind is relaxed and still.

Today's meditation phrase

The holy Christ is born in me today.

Communion question

Teacher, what does my Father Will me to know about Christ?

HEART: The skill of the heart is to make self happy. Your happiness is the most important thing in the world and cannot be sacrificed for any reason.

Today you are the ambassador of happiness. As the ambassador, your job is to demonstrate your own happiness to others and to uplift your immediate world with happy acts. Even if you don't actually feel happy, *just for today*, put on a really convincing act and pretend you're happy. Even if you have the weight of the world on your shoulders, *just for today*, act happy anyway. How many small acts of happiness can you perform for your own enjoyment and for the enjoyment of others? Make a goal to do at least 10 tangible happy acts throughout the day.

Here are some happy actions for you to consider: Smiling, saying thank you, holding the door, doing something helpful, doing something thoughtful, giving hugs, offering hope, allowing people to make mistakes and not taking offense from them, laughing, letting other drivers go first, being friendly, refraining from complaints, enjoying your work.

Write about your experience as the ambassador of happiness in your *Miracle Stopping Journal*. What did you do? How did it make you feel? How did others respond to you?

BODY: The skill of the body is to use physical tension to release physical tension.

Mode: Aerobic

Activity: Brisk walking with five 2-minute intervals of light jogging

               See below for minute-by-minute walk/jog guidelines

Time: 25 minutes

Minutes 1-3	Brisk Walking
Minute 4-5	Light Jogging
Minute 6-7	Brisk Walking
Minute 8-9	Light Jogging
Minute 10-11	Brisk Walking
Minute 12-13	Light Jogging
Minute 14-15	Brisk Walking
Minute 16-17	Light Jogging
Minute 18-19	Brisk Walking
Minute 20-21	Light Jogging
Minute 22-25	Brisk Walking

Pedometer people: Add another 250 steps today. This is + 3,500 steps from your starting point.

Write about your experience.

Day 25

LIVE WITH POWER, LOVE AND PURPOSE

Share your wisdom about the power skill of the mind

The power of decision is all that is yours. What you can decide is fixed,
because there are no alternatives except truth and illusion.

A COURSE IN MIRACLES

Every day for the past 25 days, you've been developing the skill of the mind. You
now know something about uplifting your thoughts and training your mind
that you can share with others.

* ♥ You know how to write an intention statement and how to keep changing
  it so the statement is fresh and meaningful.

* ♥ You know how to express your intention in writing, and verbally. You
  know how to use drama, fun and attitude to make your intention come
  alive.

♥ You know how to create a powerful visualization, which is a picture in your mind of what you intend to do or not do.

♥ You know how to create a stopping prayer, which is another way of asking for what you want.

♥ You know how to use your stopping intention to override conflicting and competing desires.

It's time to teach what you know and thereby learn it more fully. Today you give the lesson. Your goal is to explain how the skill of the mind enables you to stop yourself. Why should someone bother to train the mind? Start by sharing your real-life example developing intention statements and using them. Tell how training the mind made a difference for you. Explain what you do, why you do it, and what you get from it. Give simple direction that others can follow.

Set your timer for two minutes and brainstorm what you know about the skill of the mind in your *Miracle Stopping Journal*. Get your thoughts about mind down on paper, and don't worry if they're perfect or not. When you're done brainstorming, polish and refine your writing so that it's perfectly clear and others will enjoy reading it. And lastly, edit your message down to 1,000 words or less. When your message is as good as you can get it, go to www.stoppingnation.com. If you haven't already registered, do it now. Then copy and post you message in the *Wisdom of the Mind* category. Your lesson will be available for the general public to read.

DAY 25 STOPPING PRACTICE

MIND: The skill of the mind is to make a decision and hold it.

1. Write your stopping prayer in your *Miracle Stopping Journal*.

2. Shut your eyes and slowly recite it three times.

3. With your eyes shut, envision your Christ-self holding your prayer and giving it back to you as a gift that's been fulfilled.

4. With your eyes shut, envision that stopping feels like the physical sensation of fullness. Imagine this fullness penetrating your skin, flowing in your blood, seeping into your cells, and merging with your genetic code. Sit with the physical sensation of fullness for 30-60 seconds or until it dissipates.

SPIRIT: The skill of the spirit is to experience an instant of inner peace so that you can turn off the ego and connect with your Christ-self.

Today's goal is 21-minutes of meditation. You can configure your meditation time in any way that's convenient for you, but if you're inspired, consider three 7-minute meditation sessions. Asking yourself to sit in stillness three times a day is an increase in intensity of your meditation practice. As always, do your best to avoid slipping into a habitual pattern, which means don't keep using the exact same meditation pattern. Do your communion exercise after one of your long meditation periods, when your mind is relaxed and still.

Today's meditation phrase

Heaven is the decision I must make.
I make it now, and will not change my mind.

Communion question

Teacher, what does my Father Will me to know about heaven?

HEART: The skill of the heart is to make self happy. Your happiness is the most important thing in the world and cannot be sacrificed for any reason.

There's still one more technique to learn for your happiness, and it has to do with making yourself happier in your relationships. This is accomplished by doing a better and more authentic job of communicating your preferences and needs. Happiness is blocked when you have an important relationship that's out of whack. Suffering in silence is the easiest way to deal with a relationship that isn't working quite right, but it's an unsatisfying, self-destructive, and self-sacrificing solution.

Your persistent unhappiness is an attack against self that increases the proclivity to zone out in oblivion and to keep using your preferred substance. Obviously, this is not what's wanted.

You are not powerless, and your troublesome relationship is not hopeless. You can identify what you want, and you can ask for it in a loving, reasonable and peaceful way, without pitching a fit or being crazy. Revealing your essential self is an act of joining and intimacy. Intimacy is literally letting someone see *in to me.* It's a little scary because what if you muster up the courage to finally reveal your essential self, and he/she won't or can't accommodate you? Then what? We'll be working on this topic for the next few days, and that fear will be addressed. In the meantime, counter your fear by thinking of the person you identify below as completely innocent, and by that I mean, completely unaware of your unmet need. He/she is not a mind reader. He/she cannot know what you want if you don't say it. He/she cannot treat your need as important if you keep ignoring it and stifling it.

Begin the exercise by answering these two questions in your *Miracle Stopping Journal* :

1. Identify a current relationship that's troubling you. It can be a spouse, significant other, child, employer or anyone who's a big part of your world. Specify the relationship and the problem.

2. The next question is about you and only you. What need or set of needs do you have that aren't being addressed or met? Or said another way, what do you want that you're not getting? Take care not to go to the dark side, which is the slippery slope into complaining, blaming or labeling. So, for example, *my spouse is insensitive and thoughtless* is rephrased as *I need more attention and thoughtfulness from my spouse.* Or *my employer doesn't appreciate me* is rephrased as *I need more appreciation from my employer.* Or *my child only comes to me for money* is rephrased as *I need my child to come and see me just to visit.*

We'll be working on this exercise for the next couple of days. Don't worry about what comes next. Nothing is ever asked of you that you can't easily do or that you can't easily handle. Right now all you have to do is identify a troubling relationship and figure out what you want from it. That's it.

BODY: The skill of the body is to use physical tension to release physical tension.

Go to www.powertostop.com/tools for instruction if you need it.

Mode:	Strength training
Activity:	Calisthenics at home or weight training on a machine circuit at a health club
Time:	25 minutes minimum
	• 5 minutes of abdominal work
	• 10 minutes of lower body work
	• 5 minutes of upper body work
	• 5 minutes of arm work
Intensity:	Try your best to get a maximum contraction from each of your strength training moves. This is a brief, 1 or 2 second pause, at the most intense moment in the exercise.

Pedometer people: Add another 250 steps today. This is a total of + 3,500 steps from your starting point.

As always, comment on your activity experience.

Day 26

LIVE WITH POWER, LOVE AND PURPOSE

Share your wisdom about the power skill of the heart

I can elect to change all thoughts that hurt.

A COURSE IN MIRACLES

Every day for the past 26 days, you have been developing the skill of the heart. You now know something about self-love and the small effort it takes to make yourself happy that you can share with others.

♥ You know that love is harmless, God is harmless and your Christ-self is harmless. This makes you happy.

♥ You know how to forgive another, and this makes you happy.

♥ You know how to forgive yourself, and this makes you happy.

♥ You know how to express gratitude to another, and this makes you happy.

♥ You know how to express gratitude to yourself, and this makes you happy.

♥ You know your purpose and your passion, and you know that engaging in activities that reflect your purpose and passion makes you happy.

♥ You know that slowing down and giving yourself fully to any ordinary experience makes you happy.

♥ You know that acting happy and extending happiness to others makes you happy.

It's time to teach what you know and thereby learn it more fully. Today you give the lesson. Your goal is to explain why the skill of the heart enables you to love yourself and to stop yourself. Why should someone bother to learn about love and making self happy? Start by sharing your real-life example with your favorite happiness exercises. Explain how extending love and making yourself happy is up to you. Be specific about what you do, why you do it, and what you get from it. Give simple direction that others can follow.

Set your timer for two minutes and brainstorm what you know about the skill of the heart in your *Miracle Stopping Journal*. Just get your thoughts about heart down on paper, and don't worry if they're perfect or not. When you're done brainstorming, polish and refine your writing so that your message is perfectly clear and others will enjoy reading it. And lastly, edit your message down to 1,000 words or less. When your message is as good as you can get it, go to www.stoppingnation.com and post it in the *Wisdom of the Heart* category. (If you haven't already registered, you will have to do so first.) Your posted lesson will be available for the general public to read.

DAY 26 STOPPING PRACTICE

MIND: The skill of the mind is to make a decision and hold it.

1. Write your stopping prayer in your *Miracle Stopping Journal*.

2. Shut your eyes and slowly recite it three times.

3. With your eyes still shut, once again envision stopping as the sensation of fullness. Allow yourself to experience this sensation throughout your entire body. Notice the sensation expanding *beyond the border of your body*. Give yourself the experience of pushing this fullness out into the universe. Hold your awareness of expanding your fullness and of sharing it with the world for 30-60 seconds or until it dissipates.

SPIRIT: The skill of the spirit is to experience an instant of inner peace so that you can turn off the ego and connect with your Christ-self.

Today's goal is a total of 24 minutes of meditation. Configure your meditation time in any way that's convenient for you. Once again, if you're inspired, consider increasing the intensity by doing three roughly equal sessions rather than one or two. Do your communion exercise after one of your long meditation periods, when your mind is relaxed and still.

Today's meditation phrase

God is but love, and therefore so am I.

Communion question

Teacher, what does my Father Will me to know about His deep, abiding Love for me?

HEART: The skill of the heart is to make self happy. Your happiness is the most important thing in the world and cannot be sacrificed for any reason.

As you know, we're working on the identification of your need(s) and the communication of your need(s) in one of your important relationships. Yesterday you identified the relationship and you identified your need. Today you have two more goals. You're going to identify exactly what you want to happen, and you're going to brainstorm how to ask for what you want. For now, pretend that anything is possible. Don't limit yourself by what you think the person will or won't do. Think only about what you want and exactly how you'd like to get it.

1. Write down your need so that it's fresh in your mind.

2. How exactly do you want your need (or set of needs) to be met? Think of a tangible, observable way (or ways) your need can be fulfilled.

For example:

- What exactly do you want your spouse to do to express more attention?

- What exactly do you want your employer to do to demonstrate appreciation?

- What exactly do you want your child to do for or with you?

3. There are many loving, peaceful ways to express your request that don't involve yelling, getting angry, blaming, complaining or demanding. Consider the range of choices that are available to you. Some ideas are provided below, but don't limit yourself to this short list of options. The purpose of this exercise is to identify all the ways of communicating that are comfortable and natural to you. That's all. Do not act on any of these options yet.

   - I can ask for what I want, face-to-face, directly. *It would mean a lot to me if you remember my birthday next Wednesday.*

   - I can ask for what I want indirectly. I can say something like *I love it when people make a big deal out of my birthday.*

   - I can use humor. *Go ahead, make my day. My birthday's coming up and I'm daring you to do something about it!*

   - I can use prayer. *Heavenly Father, please shine a reminder of my birth into the minds of people who matter to me.*

   - I can create a beautiful visualization in my mind where I get exactly what I want. *I see myself getting cards and hugs, kisses and lots of messages on Facebook.*

   - I can create a written request that I send or don't send.

   - I can write an intention statement about getting what I want.

   - I can demonstrate what I want with my own words and with my own behavior. *I always remember birthdays of friends and family.*

   - I can commune with the Christ for help in figuring out what to do next.

4. Decide on the methodologies that feel comfortable to you. One or two will do, but again, do not act on them yet.

BODY: The skill of the body is to use physical tension to release physical tension.

Mode:	Aerobic
Activity:	Brisk walking with five 2-minute intervals of light jogging
	See below for minute-by-minute walk/jog guidelines
Time:	25 minutes

Minutes 1-3	Brisk Walking
Minute 4-5	Light Jogging
Minute 6-7	Brisk Walking
Minute 8-9	Light Jogging
Minute 10-11	Brisk Walking
Minute 12-13	Light Jogging
Minute 14-15	Brisk Walking
Minute 16-17	Light Jogging
Minute 18-19	Brisk Walking
Minute 20-21	Light Jogging
Minute 22-25	Brisk Walking

Pedometer people: Add another 250 steps today. This is + 3,750 steps from your starting point.

As always, comment on your activity experience.

Day 27

LIVE WITH POWER, LOVE AND PURPOSE

Share your wisdom about the power skill of the body

...the body should not feel at all. If you have been successful, there
will be no sense of feeling ill or feeling well, of pain or pleasure.
No response at all is in the mind to what the body does.

A COURSE IN MIRACLES

Every day for the past 27 days, you have been developing the skill of the body. You now know something that you can share with others about how to neutralize your own tension and how to transcend obsession with bodily sensations.

- ♥ You know that the body is a servant to the mind.

- ♥ You know that hateful, self-destructive thoughts in the mind produce impulsive self-destructive sensations in the body.

- ♥ You know that bodily sensations can be reinterpreted and transcended.

♥ You know that when manufactured tension is released, impulsive tension is also released.

♥ You know that basic care of the body is a demonstration of self-love.

It's time to teach what you know and thereby learn it more fully. Today you give the lesson. Your goal is to explain why the skill of the body enables you to love yourself and stop yourself. Why should you bother to take care of your body? Why should you bother to manufacture tension? Start by sharing your real-life experience with regular physical activity. Mention the variables of time, mode and intensity. Talk about the relaxation response and your personal experience with the release of tension, if any. Say what you do, when you do it and how it works for you. Give simple and clear direction that others can follow.

Set your timer for two minutes and brainstorm what you know about the skill of the body in your *Miracle Stopping Journal*. Get your thoughts about body on paper, and don't worry if they're perfect or not. When you're done brainstorming, polish and refine your writing. Get it so that others will relate to your message and enjoy what you have to say. And lastly, edit your message down to 1,000 words or less. When your message is as good as you can get it, go to www.stoppingnation.com and post it in the *Wisdom of the Body* category. (If you haven't already registered, you will have to do so first.) Your posted lesson will be available for the general public to read.

DAY 27 STOPPING PRACTICE

MIND: The skill of the mind is to make a decision and hold it.

You have had 26 days of mind training, and now it's time to direct yourself. Pick a technique for holding your intention in your mind and then implement it. Decide for yourself how many repetitions are required and how frequently you'll do them. Stand in front of a mirror and watch/listen to yourself reciting your intention at least one time. Write about your mind practice in your *Miracle Stopping Journal*.

SPIRIT: The skill of the spirit is to experience an instant of inner peace so that you can turn off the ego and connect with your Christ-self.

Today's goal is a total of 26-minutes of meditation. Configure your meditation time in any way that's convenient for you: as one session, multiple sessions, or as frequent repetitions of your meditation phrase. Don't use the same meditation pattern you used yesterday. Do your communion exercise after one of your long meditation periods, when your mind is relaxed and still.

Today's meditation phrase

Let me recognize that my problems have been solved.

Communion question

Teacher, what does my Father Will me to know about solving my stopping problem (or any other problem you'd prefer to address)?

HEART: The skill of the heart is to make self happy. Your happiness is the most important thing in the world and cannot be sacrificed for any reason.

Today we continue with the happiness practice involving the identification and communication of your unmet needs. Here's the thing to keep in mind. You are responsible for your own happiness. You can ask for what you want, but no one is obligated to please you. You can invite others to care for you in the way that you most prefer to be cared for, but ultimately, you are responsible for your own care. The thing that prevents everyone from asking for what's wanted is the fear that it won't be honored or fulfilled. Let's look at this fear directly, and then bust it.

What if you ask for something and the person can't do it or won't do it for you? Maybe you want someone in your world to be more emotionally available or responsive to you, but the person isn't in touch with his or her emotions. Consequently, he/she might not have the basic ability to meet your need. Or alternatively, he/she may simply not be inclined to do this service for you.

The preferences and abilities of one individual are preferences and abilities of one individual. It doesn't mean you can't have what you want, and it doesn't mean what you want is not available in the universe. It simply means, **what you want may not be available from this resource**. In the event your request is not honored, here are the options available to you:

1. You can open your heart and mind and calmly listen to the reason why the person in your world is unable or unwilling to respond.

2. You can ask again, perhaps with more explanation about why the need is important to you.

3. You can ask using a different methodology. (Refer to ideas from yesterday's happiness practice.)

4. You can find another resource or set of resources to fulfill your need.

5. You can stay unhappy.

6. You can change your mind about what you think you need. A need, after all, is a thought, and thoughts can be changed.

7. You can ask your Christ-self for guidance and further direction.

Fear-busting exercise:

♥ Look at these possible outcomes, and pick the one that scares you. This is the worst possible outcome. Why are you trying to avoid this outcome?

♥ Label your fear. Smile at it. Laugh at it.

♥ Instead of seeing the worst thing, envision the outcome that you want in your mind.

BODY: The skill of the body is to use physical tension to release physical tension.

If needed, go to www.powertostop.com/tools for exercise instruction.

Mode:	Flexibility
Activity:	Yoga class, DVD stretch workout, or stretching at home

Body Part: Full body

Repetitions: One or two stretches for each major joint

Intensity: Hold each stretch/pose for 10 seconds.

Pedometer people: Add another 250 steps today. This is + 4,000 steps from your starting point.

As always, comment on your activity experience.

REVIEW OF WEEK FOUR

...spirit reacts in the same way to everything it knows is true,
and does not respond at all to anything else.

A COURSE IN MIRACLES

This is your last weekly review. You're just about ready to graduate.

Week four accomplishments

♥ You progressively increased your practice of the four stopping skills.

♥ You shared your wisdom for the skill of the spirit.

♥ You shared your wisdom for the skill of the mind.

♥ You shared your wisdom for the skill of the heart.

- You shared your wisdom for the skill of the body.

- You began self-directing your daily stopping skill practice.

- You looked at an unmet need in a significant relationship, and you considered how to fulfill it.

Which weekly activity was most helpful to you?

DAY 28 STOPPING PRACTICE

MIND: The skill of the mind is to make a decision and hold it.

Direct your daily mind training. Write about your plan and your practice in your *Miracle Stopping Journal.*

SPIRIT: The skill of the spirit is to experience an instant of inner peace so that you can turn off the ego and connect with your Christ self.

Read the six meditation phrases that were provided during your second week. Pick the one that's most meaningful for you, follow the time directions associated with the phrase, and use it for your meditation today.

Write this phrase in your *Miracle Stopping Journal* and explain why it's important to you.

HEART: The skill of the heart is to make self happy. Your happiness is the most important thing in the world and cannot be sacrificed for any reason.

Resolve today to make your happiness a top priority in your own life. If you don't treat your own happiness as a priority, no one else will either. Write an intention statement about making yourself happy in your *Miracle Stopping Journal.* Here's an example.

I, _____ (insert your name), take 100% responsibility for making myself happy from this day forward. I release everyone from slavery to my happiness.

BODY: The skill of the body is to use physical tension to diffuse physical tension.

Physical rest day. No activity required.

Summarize your weekly exercise experience. Note the type of exercise you most prefer and where you see yourself headed with physical activity.

RATE YOUR 4th WEEK:

Use a scale of (1) low to (10) high. Rate your weekly experience on the program, and briefly explain why you gave this rating.

What are you doing well?

What can you do better?

Day 29

ONGOING SPIRITUAL NOURISHMENT

Consider A Course In Miracles

...the attraction of love for love remains irresistible.
For it is the function of love to unite all things unto itself.

A COURSE IN MIRACLES

Ongoing spiritual training in love and harmlessness is highly recommended. Otherwise, by default, ego will continue to dominate your thoughts, which will continue to drive your behavior in self-destructive ways. Few spiritual works exist that exclusively teach harmlessness, where no degrees of judgment, anger or guilt are desirable. Many current and bestselling works blend pop psychology ideas with spiritual concepts. Most typically, *a little* judgment is perceived as essential and justified, and *a little* anger or guilt is erroneously perceived as appropriate and helpful. This is very confusing, and it compromises a key idea that 100% harmlessness is essential for self-navigation. *A Course In Miracles* is preferred and recommended because spiritual principles are not watered down and made more

190

socially acceptable. I personally like that it offers a godly but non-religious ideology dedicated to transcending ego. It's also the only spiritual resource available that offers a disciplined, do-it-yourself 365-day mind training program.

A Course In Miracles is known by the acronym, *ACIM*, and it's also referred to as the *Course*. Technically, the *Course* is a set of three different books that are packaged and sold as one complete unit. There's a *Text*, which explains a new and non-religious thought system about God, the world, and our role in it. There's a *Workbook*, which, as mentioned above, gives the reader 365 daily lessons for retraining the mind and restoring divine connection. And there's a *Manual for Teachers* for anyone who's inspired to share the miracle of transformation and healing that's received.

The *Course* uses familiar Judeo-Christian terminologies like Christ, Father, Holy Spirit, Atonement and others, but the *Course* is not a religion, and it does not teach Jewish or Christian theology. There is no church to attend, no rules to follow, no leaders who are not your equal, no sacraments, no rituals, no organization or group to join, no donation to make. In fact, reading the *Course* and taking daily *Course* lessons can be done completely on your own with only your inner teacher/ Christ-self to provide guidance.

The controversy surrounding the Course is that it's a channeled work. This means it was received and transcribed by two ordinary humans, Helen Schucman and Bill Thetford, but it was not authored by a human ego mind. The content is simply too loving, too radiant, too exquisitely beautiful to come from anything except a divine Source. After you read the *Course* for a little while, it becomes clear that the author is Jesus. This is one of those statements that sounds wak-a-doodle, implausible and completely over-the-top, and it's why you need to read it for yourself. After you have the direct, personal experience of being deeply inspired by Jesus, you can form your own conclusion. Jesus presents himself as an equal brother, not a sensational superstar who asks for your worship or who demands your allegiance. He is freely available to all who seek a wholly loving path to God.

> This Course has come from him because his words have reached
> you in a language you can love and understand. Are other teachers
> possible, to lead the way to those who speak in different tongues and
> appeal to different symbols? Certainly there are...Jesus has come to
> answer yours. In Him you find God's answer.

My favorite way to explain the *Course* is to say it's a guide to heaven for all who wish to go. Heaven is that perfect state of mind where love is continually experienced and extended. Nothing is needed and nothing is wanted except to be the loving being that you are. The *Course* teaches how to have a more loving life experience, how to be a more loving being, and how to accept and receive more love from others. Love is our true nature, but it's covered up by ego and forgotten. Consequently, the task is to undo the blocks to love. We learn that happiness depends on extending love to self and others, no matter what.

- ♥ If the thoughts in your mind are making you miserable and you want to change them, consider *A Course In Miracles.* Your mind will be changed.

- ♥ If you want to like what you see when you look in the mirror, consider *A Course In Miracles.* Your vision will improve.

- ♥ If you need a miracle or a healing in your life, consider *A Course In Miracles.* Miracles are your birthright.

- ♥ If you want to find love in yourself and others, consider *A Course In Miracles.* You are the love you seek. This is the path to and of Love. Love is the only thing that really matters.

> When I said "I come as the light of the world," I meant that I came
> to share the light with you....If my light goes with you everywhere,
> you shine it away with me.
>
> You have been asked to take me as your model for learning,
> since an extreme example is a particularly helpful learning device...
> You are merely asked to follow my example in the face of much less
> extreme temptations to misperceive, and not to accept them as false
> justifications for anger.

I elected, for your sake and mine, to demonstrate that the most outrageous assault, as judged by the ego, does not matter.

I do not call for martyrs but for teachers.

I have made it perfectly clear that I am like you and you are like me, but our fundamental equality can be demonstrated only through joint decision.

Your mission is very simple. You are asked to live so as to demonstrate you are not an ego, and I do not choose God's channels wrongly.

...those who accept me as a model are literally my disciples.

A Course In Miracles can be purchased at Amazon.com, at most large book stores, and at a discounted price at www.miracles-course.org.

DAY 29 STOPPING PRACTICE

MIND: The skill of the mind is to make a decision and hold it.

Direct your own mind training today. Pick a technique for holding your intention in your mind and implement it. Decide for yourself how many repetitions are required and how frequently you'll do them. Write about your stopping practice in your *Miracle Stopping Journal.*

SPIRIT: The skill of the spirit is to experience an instant of inner peace so that you can turn off the ego and connect with your Christ-self.

Today's goal is a total of 30-minutes of meditation. Configure your meditation time in any way that's convenient for you: as one session, multiple sessions, or as frequent repetitions of your meditation phrase. Do your communion exercise after one of your long meditation periods, when your mind is relaxed and still.

Today's meditation phrase

The Holy Spirit speaks through me today.

Communion question

Teacher, what does my Father Will me to know about my ongoing spiritual nourishment?

HEART: The skill of the heart is to make self happy. Your happiness is the most important thing in the world and cannot be sacrificed for any reason.

You have now had 28 days of practice with different techniques for making yourself happy. Happiness is your job. Direct yourself. What will you do to make yourself happy today? Write your plan in your *Miracle Stopping Journal* and then comment on your actual effort compared to your plan.

BODY: The skill of the body is to use physical tension to release physical tension.

Mode:	Aerobic
Activity:	Light jogging with 6 intervals of brisk walking
Time:	30 minutes

Minutes 1-3	Brisk Walking
Minute 4-5-6	Light Jogging
Minute 7-8	Brisk Walking
Minute 9-10-11	Light Jogging
Minute 12-13	Brisk Walking
Minute 14-15-16	Light Jogging
Minute 17-18	Brisk Walking

Minute 19-20-21	Light Jogging
Minute 22-23	Brisk Walking
Minute 24-25-26	Light Jogging
Minute 27-30	Brisk Walking

Pedometer people: Add another 250 steps today. This is + 4,250 steps from your starting point.

As always, comment on your activity experience in your *Miracle Stopping Journal.*

Day 30

MORE NOURISHMENT

Eleven inspirational resources

You do not walk alone. God's angels hover near and all about. His Love
surrounds you, and of this be sure; that I will never leave you comfortless.
A COURSE IN MIRACLES

B ooks provide you with the easiest and most reliable way to keep pumping
wholesome, nourishing ideas into your mind. Put the books mentioned below
on your reading list, and then keep them in your reference library as a handy
resource. Of course, there are many other worthwhile books that aren't suggested
here. My recommendation list is deliberately kept short because I want to improve
the chances that you'll actually buy these books and read them. The authors are all
established pros with a long-term track record. Each book is a gem -- jam-packed
with practical, doable ideas anyone can implement.

BRAD BLANTON
www.radicalhonesty.com
Radical Honesty

Blanton is completely irreverent, and he's fond of using the f-word, which I like. I also like that Blanton has no secrets. He puts himself on the table, and you either take him or leave him. Blanton's greatest therapeutic strength is his razor-sharp clarity and his rare ability to quickly cut through all the BS and social games we like to play. He believes, for example, that healing is only possible when you're not hiding. This is actually a deeply spiritual principle, but Blanton presents it from a psychological perspective. *We all lie like hell. It wears us out. It is the major source of all human stress.* Truth-telling, in contrast, is a giant release of energy. Instead of withholding your truth, you express it. The person who's most capable of intimacy and connecting with others is the person who's most capable of telling the truth. *When, through telling the truth, you destroy an illusion, you can then see that it was meaningless.*

One very small caution about *Radical Honesty*. Blanton says anger is essential for getting to truth, but it's not. Truth can be revealed without making someone else bad or wrong, and problems can be resolved without anger. Anger is the common ego default response to every disappointment, but it can be transcended.

CARLOS CASTANEDA
The Teachings Of Don Juan
A Separate Reality
Journey To Ixtlan
The Fire From Within
Power Of Silence
The Active Side Of Infinity

Castaneda's work is best read as a series, in the order listed, rather than as a single book. The books recount Castaneda's personal experiences as an apprentice with a Mexican man of knowledge Castaneda calls don Juan Mateus. A man of knowledge is an egoless or enlightened being who lives, selflessly, as a conduit for Spirit. Castaneda wrote these books over a 30 year period, from 1968 to 1998, from the time he was a PhD candidate in anthropology at UCLA until the year he died. His great but underrated service to humanity is the diligent capturing of don Juan's words in his field notes. Don Juan's wisdom is then relayed to us in an easy-to-understand conversational format in affordable books. There are/were very few enlightened beings here on Earth, and don Juan was one of them.

That said, Castaneda's work is controversial. Academic circles call him a fraud and a charismatic cult leader. Ignore the drama, and overlook Castaneda's initial fascination with hallucinogenic drugs. None of it matters. The extraordinary wisdom from don Juan cannot be faked. In spite of himself, Castaneda inadvertently further demonstrates authenticity through his incomplete story-telling. It takes Castaneda several years to fully comprehend and appreciate what he stumbled on with don Juan. Because of this, Castaneda never quite gets around to explaining don Juan's thought system in a whole or organized way, but the series is still monumentally worth reading. Castaneda's many conversations with don Juan are like nuggets of gold that offer insights into a thought system that's been lost and is not otherwise available to us.

By the way, Castaneda revolutionized anthropological field work practices. Rather than observing and reporting as an observer, Castaneda directly participated and reported as a participant. This was never done before. His books sold over ten million copies, a rare and distinguished accomplishment, and are still available in multiple languages around the world.

CHOGYAM TRUNGPA
Shambhala: The Sacred Path of the Warrior

Chogyam Trungpa was born in 1939 in Tibet and was quickly recognized as a religiously important re-incarnated being (the 11th Trungpa Tulku). Unfortunately for us, Chogyam Trungpa didn't stick around on the planet very long, and he died at young age of 44 in Halifax, Canada. When he was just 20, Chogyam Trungpa followed the lead of the Dalai Lama and trekked across the Himalayas by foot from Tibet to India. This is where he learned how to speak English. Eleven years later Chogyam Trungpa moved to Boulder, Colorado where he founded Naropa Institute, the first fully accredited Buddhist university in North America. Chogyam

Trungpa is well known for establishing over 100 meditation centers worldwide and for writing extensively on Buddhism. Many of his beautifully written books are still in my library, and this is why I eagerly purchased *Shambhala*, Chogyam Trungpa's masterpiece.

Shambhala is the mythical enlightened society in the Himalayas. Chogyam Trungpa invites us to create our own Shambhala by discovering what we each inherently have to offer the world to uplift human existence. The essential revelation of self is an act of bravery, and the people who live without deception are warriors. While warriorhood is explained in a way that's appealing and relevant to Westerners, *Shambhala* has more to offer than easily digestible sound-bytes for Americans. It's a radical reinterpretation of Buddhism, but completely without Buddhism. Just like there are many different sects of Christians, there are also different sects of Buddhists, and this can be confusing to those who are unfamiliar with the religion. *Shambhala* presents the reader with a reason to be good and to do good for the sake of warriorhood. The prospect of experiencing your own goodness will set your heart on fire.

CHRIS CROWLEY
www.youngernextyear.com
Younger Next Year (with Henry S. Lodge, M.D.)
Younger Next Year for Women (with Henry S. Lodge, M.D.)

Okay, I have a bias. When it comes to Chris Crowley, I'm like a gushing 14-year old with a crush on a rock star. Crowley's infectious *stay alive* message pulls me into his orb like a moth to a flame, and it will pull you too. Even though Crowley is a 70-something guy, he's still fit, hunky and hungry for life. He's part coach, part zealous missionary for fitness, part role model, part friend and full of hope and inspiration. There's a very big difference between a sedentary, depressed, sickly lifestyle and an active one. Crowley not only demonstrates how to become fit at any age of life, his power of persuasion is strong enough to lift you right off the couch. *Younger Next Year* is the Bible for using physical activity as a tool to slow down the aging process and stay alive. Crowley and Lodge explain precisely what to do and why you should do it. Lodge gives the scientific rational, but it's Crowley who wins you over with his personal stories and pep talks. I first got turned onto *Younger Next*

Year when I read somewhere that President Obama had a copy of it in his gym bag. Get one for your gym bag, too.

DON MIGUEL RUIZ
www.miguelruiz.com
The Four Agreements
The Mastery of Love

Don Miguel Ruiz is a Mexican healer, shaman and surgeon who teaches the Toltec Way of Wisdom. It's similar to the ideology taught by don Juan in the Castaneda series, but without the ruthlessness and sweeping sense of wonder. Ruiz provides a guide to freedom based on truth and common sense. In T*he Four Agreements* we learn four rules for a lifestyle that's more functional and less disappointing. 1) Be impeccable with your word. 2) Don't take anything personally. 3) Don't make assumptions. 4) Always do your best. In *The Mastery of Love,* Ruiz explains why love is the only thing that matters, especially love of self, which involves taking responsibility for your own happiness. All relationships with others start with you and how you feel about yourself. We allow as much abuse or emotional pain from others as we inflict upon self. A truly loving relationship requires self-love.

ESTHER AND JERRY HICKS (The Teachings of Abraham)
www.abraham-hicks.com
Ask and It Is Given

Esther Hicks receives the channeled teachings of Abraham, the name for a collection of higher beings with pure, positive energy dedicated to serving all humanity. Their works are generally referred to as *Abraham-Hicks* to reflect that Esther, Jerry (Esther's husband) and Abraham willingly and mindfully collaborate in the writing process and in sharing their message. Everything put out by Abraham-Hicks is helpful, and I had a hard time deciding which books to recommend. Really, you could pick anything from them. I finally decided to draw your attention to *Ask and It Is Given*, an early book, because it explains the law of attraction and how to use it. The law of attraction is based on the simple, but powerful idea that like things attract because they have the same kind of energy. So if you want to manifest something in your life, you must first be like it before it will come to you.

The attraction process is relatively easy to master. First you have to notice your current vibrational frequency, which is accomplished by paying attention to your emotional state of mind. Then you have to fine-tune or change your vibrational frequency to match to what's wanted. This is done by changing your thought (and holding the new thought) to uplift the way you feel. So, for example, if you're feeling angry or sad, you have to correct the underlying thought that's making you angry or sad. Otherwise you'll draw more anger and sadness to yourself. *The way you feel is a clear and accurate indication of your alignment or misalignment with your Source Energy.*

JOEL GOLDSMITH
www.joelgoldsmith.com
The Infinite Way
The Art of Spiritual Healing

Goldsmith was born in New York City in 1892 to non-practicing Jewish parents. Not much is known about him until 1928 when Goldsmith, then 36, was cured of a serious health problem (possibly tuberculosis) by a Christian Scientist. Goldsmith converted to Christian Science, moved to Boston and practiced at the Christian Science Mother Church for the next 16 years. It's unlikely Goldsmith would have known Mary Baker Eddy, the founder of Christian Science, because she died in 1910. That said, he was strongly influenced by Eddy's work and by her extraordinary track record as a miracle healer.

Goldsmith's *Infinite Way* message was received *through him* in the 1940's and became the foundation for his lifework as a spiritual teacher and healer. While Goldsmith makes references to Jesus and uses other Christian terms in his books, he doesn't teach religion and he doesn't align himself with any religion. There is no dogma, no ceremony, no ritual. Instead, Goldsmith advocates the power of meditation, deep communion with God, and getting out of God's way so He can do his work through you. Quite simply, if you want to experience the grace of God, you must align yourself with God. Goldsmith's writing style has an old-fashioned tone, but his message is timeless. There's a rumor floating around on the internet that people who read *The Art of Spiritual Healing* are spontaneously healed, and I hope it's true. I particularly like *The Art of Spiritual Healing* because Goldsmith gives explicit direction about how he performs a spiritual healing.

MOTHER MEERA
www.mothermeeradarshan.org/
Mother Meera Answers
Mother Meera Answers Part II

An avatar is the Hindu name for the human embodiment or incarnation of Divine energy. Mother Meera is the avatar of the Divine Mother or Shakti, and her Earthly mission is to activate the light that comes from God and make it available to us. This activation of light accelerates spiritual growth and makes it easier for us to undo the blocks that are holding us back. Born in South India in 1960, Mother Meera now lives in Dornburg-Thalheim Germany where she provides a service called a Darshan, which is available for free to anyone who wants it. Thousands of people from all over the world come to visit Mother Meera and to participate in her Darshan. The Darshan is conducted completely in silence so that God's light can be energized and transmitted to all who are present. There is no lecturing or teaching. Instead, Mother Meera touches each attendee and looks in his or her eyes. Mother Meera is not associated with any religion. The only practice Mother Meera advocates is called *japa*, the silent repetition of any divine name such as Jesus, over and over, to activate God's light.

SANAYA ROMAN
www.orindaben.com
Personal Power through Awareness
Living with Joy
Spiritual Growth

In the 1980's Sanaya Roman wrote a series of books that were channeled to her by Orin, a higher being. My personal favorites are listed here, but Roman offers other books and products that are also worth checking out. Orin has a refreshingly light and gentle touch in the way that he explains spiritual principles. This makes it easy and enjoyable to follow along, and his advice feels like a natural, common sense thing to do. Orin is also highly practical, and he uses concrete examples as well as *play* exercises to show how to apply the spiritual lessons in everyday life. The idea that we're precise energy-sensing devices is one of his key teachings. This is similar to the message from Abraham-Hicks, but it came out almost 20 years earlier. Orin's ultimate goal is to help us become inner directed so that we can more consciously decide a path of action rather than having our thoughts determined by the energy that's around us. Orin says we reach a major turning point when we take full responsibility for everything that happens to us. People feel more powerful and in control of life when they learn how to create whatever is wanted. Following and trusting your intuition puts you in touch with a higher energy flow and will bring about faster, better results than following a to do list.

SHANE CLAIBORNE
www.thesimpleway.org/shane/
The Irresistible Revolution

Shane Claiborne's passion for love is so magnetic, I seriously considered jumping on a plane and flying down to inner city Philadelphia just to meet him and absorb his loving presence. Claiborne is 100% devoted to living *The Simple Way*, and the goals are truly simple. Love God. Love people. Follow Jesus. His radical, reinterpretation of Christianity is fresh, vibrant and compelling, and people who prefer a literal or more traditional interpretation may not like it. *It was like we had brought something dead back to life…God forgive us for all those we have lost because we made the Gospel boring. It's because we make the Gospel too easy, not because we make it too difficult.*

Claiborne, who is still a relatively young man, started out in life as an über-traditional born-again Christian on the fast track to scooping up religious fame and a wife-for-life. Then something truly revolutionary happened to him. He discovered that church isn't a stained glass window or a structure. Rather, it's the love you have in your heart for God and for others, especially people who are suffering from poverty. Claiborne spent time with Mother Teresa in Calcutta before she died, and was greatly influenced by her devotion to God and her selfless willingness to serve the poor. He believes growth and happiness is achieved by living in a *heroic* way where you allow yourself to be touched and moved by the suffering of others.

THADDEUS GOLAS
The Lazy Man's Guide to Enlightenment

The Lazy Man's Guide to Enlightenment is a tiny book you can quickly read in an hour. It's easily overlooked as a non-serious work for LSD users, but don't overlook it. Golas lived from 1924 to 1997. He wrote *The Lazy Man's Guide to Enlightenment* in 1971 at the height of the hippie psychedelic drug era. Originally, it was intended to be a helpful guide when you're *stuck in a weird place*, but it evolved into a world-class epistle on enlightenment. The existential question Golas asks is *how did you lock yourself into a body and play games on the material plane. And how did you get others to agree to the same game?*

Golas masterfully consolidates his ideas about freedom, reality, resistance and love into ten succinct chapters that will leave you wanting to read more. He explains that we're all completely equal, and he was the first to introduce the concept of life experience being determined by vibrational level. (This is the same concept later more fully developed by both Orin and Abraham-Hicks.) No one can help or hurt anyone without their personal agreement to play the game, so to speak. Golas says there are many paths to enlightenment, but the one that's available to everyone is love.

DAY 30 STOPPING PRACTICE

MIND: The skill of the mind is to make a decision and hold it

Direct your own mind training today. Pick a technique for holding your intention in your mind and implement it. Decide for yourself how many repetitions are required and how frequently you'll do them. Write about your stopping affirmation/intention plan and practice in your *Miracle Stopping Journal*.

SPIRIT: The skill of the spirit is to experience an instant of inner peace so that you can turn off the ego and connect with your Christ-self.

Today's goal is 30-minutes of meditation. Configure your meditation time in any way that's convenient for you: as one session, multiple sessions, or as frequent repetitions of your meditation phrase. Don't use the same meditation pattern you used yesterday. Do your communion exercise after one of your long meditation periods, when your mind is relaxed and still.

Today's meditation phrase

I give the miracles I have received.

Communion question

Teacher, what does my Father Will me to know about miracles?

HEART: The skill of the heart is to make self happy. Your happiness is the most important thing in the world and cannot be sacrificed for any reason.

Think about this for a moment. What if you really and truly are a miracle worker? What suffering would you end? How would you use your power to serve others? Why does the prospect of performing miracles get you excited and energized? Use this last day to consider and write about the possibility of doing miracle work and the relationship of miracle work to your happiness.

BODY: The skill of the body is to use physical tension to release physical tension.

Mode:	Aerobic
Activity:	Light jogging with 6 intervals of brisk walking
Time:	30 minutes

Minutes 1-3	Brisk Walking
Minute 4-5-6	Light Jogging
Minute 7-8	Brisk Walking
Minute 9-10-11	Light Jogging
Minute12-13	Brisk Walking
Minute 14-15-16	Light Jogging
Minute 17-18	Brisk Walking
Minute 19-20-21	Light Jogging
Minute 22-23	Brisk Walking
Minute 24-25-26	Light Jogging
Minute 27-30	Brisk Walking

Pedometer people: Add another 250 steps today. This is + 4,500 steps from your starting point.

As always, comment on your activity experience in your *Miracle Stopping Journal.*

GUIDELINES FOR OUT-OF-CONTROL EATERS

The solution for out-of-control eating is based on ending the bio-chemical reliance on sugar, caloric sweeteners and other substances (that quickly convert to sugar in the blood stream) to provide oblivion, comfort and release from tension. Five easy guidelines are provided below.

1. Normalize your eating pattern to 5 or 6 eating occasions per day. This is a generous boundary that anyone can easily live with. Eating occasions consist of three meals and two or three snacks per day.

2. Do not allow yourself to get hungry. Hunger <u>always</u> provokes crazy eating. Excluding sleeping time, do not go more than 4 hours without eating.

3. Eliminate all caloric sweeteners and highly processed flours from your diet. These are the foods that create bio-chemical cravings and that lead to binge eating.

    Caloric sweeteners include these common substances:

    Sugar (all types - raw, organic, brown, sucrose, etc.)

    High fructose corn syrup (HFCS)

    Syrup of any kind including agave syrup

    Molasses

    Honey

Fruit juices and concentrated fruit juices

Sugar alcohols, especially maltitol (the sweetening agent found in most sugarfree foods)

Malt or maltose

Highly processed flours include these common substances:

White flour (also known as wheat flour or enriched flour)

Corn flour

Rice flour

Corn starch

NOTE: Up to 2 ounces of whole grains per day are allowed, but be aware that wheat products, whether they're whole or refined, provoke binge-eating behaviors in some *(but not all)* people.

4. Use the *Rule of Four* when making a purchase decision about anything that comes in a package. The *Rule of Four* reminds you to count the first four <u>food </u>ingredients in a recipe. **Note that water, herbs, spices, and chemicals are <u>not</u> foods.** The basic idea is to choose packaged products where caloric sweeteners or highly processed flours are the 4th food ingredient or farther down on the ingredients list. The 4th food ingredient position indicates a low concentration of the substance, which means there's not enough of it in the recipe to worry about. Look for the ingredients list on the back or the side of the product package. Sometimes it's under a flap.

5. Dietary fat is your friend. That's right. It's your friend, and you deliberately want to include fat in some of your food choices. Fat fills you up, it satisfies you, and it normalizes and minimizes food cravings. For you, caloric sweeteners are the thing to avoid, and fat is okay, especially healthy fats like olive oil.

If you're interested in losing weight along with stopping your out-of-control eating behavior, please consider my SugarFreeMiracle™ Diet System, which was written specifically for out-of-control eaters. This easy-to-follow program is available instantly through PDF download at www.sugarfreemiracle.com

Day by day, day by day,
Oh Dear Lord three things I pray.
To see Thee more clearly,
To love Thee more dearly,
Follow Thee more nearly
Day by day

From the Musical GODSPELL
Music by Stephen Schwartz
Lyrics by Richard of Chichester (1197-1253)

Printed in the USA
CPSIA information can be obtained
at www.ICGtesting.com
JSHW080848110624
64553JS00005B/386